# Letters From
# South Caicos

## TWO YEARS LIVING THE ISLAND DREAM

*(March 24, 1974 - December 1, 1975)*

## KATHERINE ORR

South Caicos
Heritage
Foundation

South Caicos, Turks and Caicos Islands

ISBN 978-1-7354042-6-4

Second Edition

Printed in the United States of America

Cover, book design, and maps: Laurie Goralka Design

Illustrations by Katherine Orr

Photos were taken by the Orr family, except for:

Cover: *Alondra* under sail in South Caicos Harbour by
    Vern Zagornik

Boiling Hole (page 38) by Diane Taylor

Published by the South Caicos Heritage Foundation

Front Street

South Caicos

Turks and Caicos Islands

TKCA 1ZZ

southcaicosheritagefoundation.com

# Table of Contents

# Preface

OLD LETTERS bring the past to life in a unique way. They convey a sense of the dailiness of things by describing lived experience on a personal level.

These letters provide a window into a place and time gone by. In the early 1970s, an adventure at sea led the author to South Caicos, a small island where tall mounds of salt still gleamed in the sun and conchs were plentiful in the shallows of the harbor. As if frozen in permafrost and recently thawed, these personal letters—intentional memoirs—stand as an account of what was. Taken altogether, they provide an intriguing look back into an extraordinary time on a special island for those ready and willing to take the journey.

In 1972, I was a graduate student in zoology at the University of Connecticut (UConn). I was looking for a project to fulfill my master's degree that was relevant, practical, fun and also fundable. I learned that the National Park Service on St. John, U.S. Virgin Islands, had a fisheries question in need of an answer. Local fishermen were being cited for poaching queen conchs within the park, but the fishermen denied wrongdoing. They said their catch was fished legally because conchs migrated seasonally beyond the park's protective boundaries. The Park Service didn't know what was true: Did these snails migrate as the fishermen claimed? To me—an avid scuba diver and nature lover—the opportunity to answer this question seemed thrilling and doable. I began making plans…

By November of 1973, with grant funding from UConn, I was headed to the islands to unravel the mystery. I was with my partner, Chuck Hesse, aboard his 28-foot wooden sailing ketch, *Alondra*. We were bound for the Virgins—or so we thought—until fate intervened and led us to South Caicos.

This collection of letters takes readers on a journey from Biscayne Bay through the (almost) two years we lived on South Caicos. Written to my parents and shared with my sister Alison and six year old brother Chris, the original letters were scribed in longhand on lined yellow sheets of paper, often with scratch outs and quick sketches in the margins. A close friend of my mother hand typed them for safekeeping. I added more complete sketches as the book came into being. My parents and sister took the photographs during their visits in 1974 and 1975. The following maps locate South Caicos, Turks and Caicos Islands, and show the route we sailed to get there.

# Acknowledgments

To Colin Kihnke—thank you for your vision of creating this book, and for providing the support to make it happen. Your enthusiasm for all things South and your dedication to the island and its people inspired me to want to join in your cause.

To Chris Buys—my humble thanks for your steadfast encouragement and faith in my abilities. Your helpful comments and suggestions have kept me motivated and on track throughout this journey.

To Laurie Goralka Casselberry—my grateful appreciation for your lovely design and layout. Your professional expertise and artistry have transformed a daunting collection of letters, sketches, photos and other moving parts into a seamless whole.

Colin, Chris, and Laurie...working with you has been an honor and a pleasure. Without you three, there would be no book.

To Bonnie Beach—thank you for your much-needed editorial skills. Your good work has made this book better.

To my friends and loved ones who have seen various parts of the manuscript and given me their thoughts and suggestions—thank you for your time and caring.

My thanks and appreciation also go to Chuck and all the people in South Caicos and Grand Turk who welcomed us, housed us, and made my research possible.

Last but not least, I give a nod to my old friend Serendipity. Were it not for you sending Colin my way, these letters from South Caicos would still be tucked away in an old storage box.

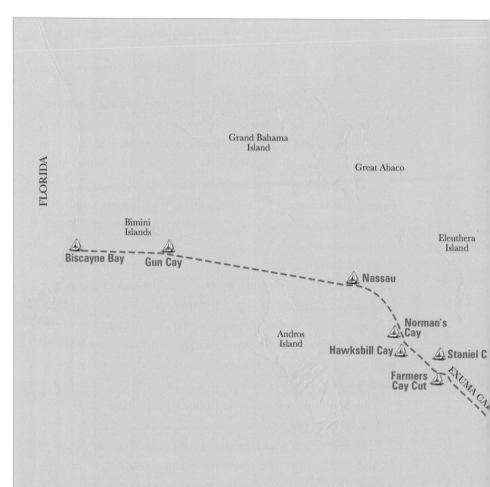

# *ALONDRA'S* SAILING ROUTE FROM BISCAYNE BAY TO SOUTH CAICOS
### *(February 22—March 24, 1974)*

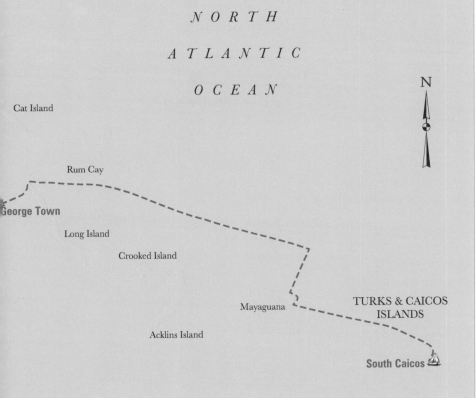

*N O R T H*

*A T L A N T I C*

*O C E A N*

N

Cat Island

Rum Cay

George Town

Long Island

Crooked Island

Mayaguana

TURKS & CAICOS
ISLANDS

Acklins Island

South Caicos

**Cockburn Harbour
Area enlarged**

Conch Ground    Admiral's
●Arms Hotel

Government●
Fisheries Building

Dove Cay
●

**The Wall
Dive Site**

Middleton
Cay

Conch
Study Site
●

Six Hill Cays

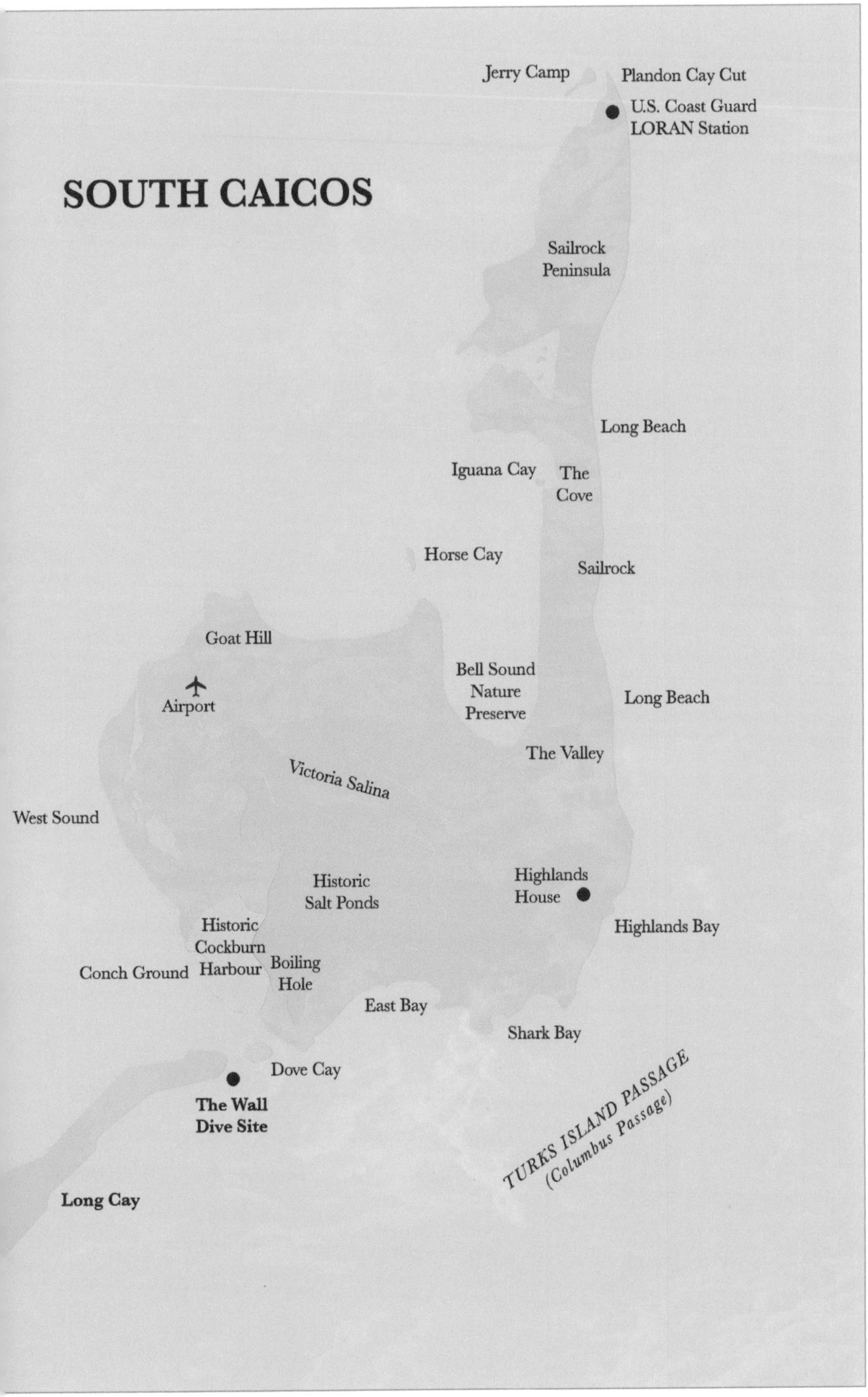

# SOUTH CAICOS

Jerry Camp

Plandon Cay Cut

U.S. Coast Guard
LORAN Station

Sailrock
Peninsula

Long Beach

Iguana Cay

The
Cove

Horse Cay

Sailrock

Goat Hill

Airport

Bell Sound
Nature
Preserve

Long Beach

The Valley

Victoria Salina

West Sound

Historic
Salt Ponds

Highlands
House

Highlands Bay

Historic
Cockburn
Harbour

Conch Ground

Boiling
Hole

East Bay

Shark Bay

Dove Cay

**The Wall
Dive Site**

**Long Cay**

TURKS ISLAND PASSAGE
*(Columbus Passage)*

# The
# Letters

*April 3, 1974*

*Dear Mom & Dad,*

We seem to have arrived! Not in the Virgins, of course, but we seem to have arrived, nonetheless. Although the events of the last few days are more than enough to fill a good-sized letter by themselves, I want to bring you up to date on our adventures since leaving Biscayne Bay on February 22nd. Aside from serving as my own record of our trip (so please hang onto these letters for me), the following account will help you understand how we got to South Caicos. From there, I'll build my case for why I think we should stay.

Winter weather can be unpredictable, so our decision for when to cross the Gulf Stream to the Bahamas

was a *yes* one minute, *no* the next, and then somehow we were off. The wind had been blowing out of the south all morning—a sure sign of a front, and just what we wanted to boost us across the Gulf Stream. But one never knows what *kind* of front it is without trying it. People in Florida who are coast sailors make sort of a big deal about crossing the Stream because of its strong northward current (up to 6 knots midstream), which tends to be choppy and, by all reports, must never be crossed in an opposing north wind. We found a little article in *Sail Magazine*, however, that presented a nifty cookbook formula on how much drift to compensate for over x hours at y speed to end up where you want in what direction of wind. We had decided to go to Gun Cay instead of Bimini because, with a northerly set, if we missed Gun Cay we'd reach Bimini; but if we missed Bimini, it would be a long way back down the coast of Florida for a second try.

So off we went—and had a fantastic sail! Sunny, fine breeze and brilliant turquoise water until suddenly we hit the deep midnight blue of the Gulf Stream. Schools of flying fish leaped not far from our bow, and a few Portuguese man–o'-wars drifted by. I saw a good-sized shark cruising lazily along the surface and got so excited about it that I lost the earpiece off my sunglasses.

By night, the water nearly glowed with phosphorescence as starry as the sky. At 11 p.m. we spotted Bimini light. We were right on course to Gun Cay light, which became visible shortly thereafter. That was the good news. The bad news was that a black line of darkness that obscured the stars was creeping up behind us.

We, and the frontline of the northeaster, arrived at Gun Cay simultaneously around 2 a.m. The wind rapidly (in a matter of minutes) swung from SW through to NE and unleashed all manner of rain, wind and wrath. The initial cloudburst was so intense I could not see my out-stretched hand in front of my face, and the sound of crashing waves on the rocky bluff of Gun Cay was lost in the general din of driving rain. Fortunately, we were near enough to throw out our storm anchor and 100 feet of chain, wait for it to grab the bottom securely and ride it out safely (albeit bucking like a bronco) 'til dawn.

The following morning was sparkling and sunny, with no hint of the passing front but a rolling swell and a gentle NE wind. Gun Cay was a lovely bit of island— nothing but scrubby hills in all shades of green with spat-terings of palm trees, grey volcanic-looking sandstone rock shores, and a beautiful little pastel-pink lighthouse perched on the hill. The water here was, as we were to find throughout the Bahamas, absolutely crystal clear— more so than anywhere in Venezuela or the Virgins as I remember them—living up to their reputation as some of the clearest waters in the world.

After a day of catching up on sleep, some snorkeling and sketching, we headed off toward Nassau across the Bahamas Bank—a two-day trip out of sight of land, yet shallow water (a few fathoms) most of the way. We anchored that night for about six hours of sleep. How amazing to be anchored while out of sight of land! My amazement didn't end there, either. When Chuck hauled in the anchor next morning, he found a bit of old line encrusted with algae snagged on the anchor tines. I was cooking our breakfast when he called me on deck. "Shall we see what's at the end of it?" he asked. He proceeded to pull, while I coiled what turned out to be 100 feet of sturdy anchor line, followed by a lovely plough anchor and chain. Plough anchors are perfect for certain kinds of soft substrate. We'd wanted to pick up a plough for our collection, and here we were, quite literally "picking

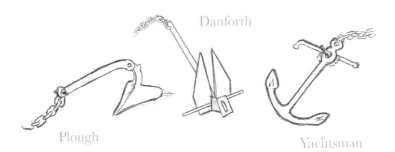

Danforth

Plough

Yachtsman

one up" off the sea bottom while out of sight of land. What's more, it was the perfect size and weight for our boat! Now we always double anchor with both our Danforth and the plough, leaving our 50-pound Yachtsman for bad weather use only. (Double anchoring is standard procedure due to tidal currents in the Bahamas.)

Our landfall at Nassau the following night was no less dramatic than the one at Gun Cay. The day's sail had been brisk and pleasant—both exhilarating and yet so peaceful to see nothing but ocean and sky from horizon to horizon. We approached New Providence by late afternoon, but we had a good 20 miles or so to run down the coast before reaching Nassau's harbor. At dusk, we began looking for the navigation beacons listed in our cruising guide to give us our bearings. Oddly, the lights we spotted (identified by color and frequency) were not listed, while we couldn't find those that were. Meanwhile, another northeaster was building up behind us. So on we sailed in darkness, amid rising winds and seas, looking for lights that didn't seem to be there. We passed rocky outcrops of reef, visible in the dark only as black silhouettes against the lights along shore. (This could get very dramatic, but I'll leave it at that.)

As we reached the lights that, though unlisted, had to be the harbor, Chuck managed to decipher the whole mess, and we slipped around a breakwater into calm waters and a welcome anchorage. It turned out that the (listed) 10-second light was flashing at 5 seconds; the 5-second light was actually flashing at 8-second intervals, and we never saw the green harbor light because it wasn't lit. In fact, as we entered the harbor, we passed three buoys that loomed as dark shapes in front of us before their feebly flickering lights could be seen. Some welcome to Nassau.

That night it really blew a gale and next morning, still blowing, we watched a hundred-or-so racing yachts come into the harbor. These boats were finishing the Miami-Nassau race (Southern Atlantic Racing Circuit: SARC), 140 boats in all (actually, 139 after one hit a reef). These yachts tied up customs for the day, so we waited until the following day to check in and go ashore.

It was easy to lose a few days in Nassau writing post-cards, picking up supplies, exploring the old fortress and straw market, buying bananas down by the wharf and watching the conch fishermen prepare their catch to be dried. Even the harbor had clear water that offered a bit of interesting snorkeling. We were fascinated by the many Haitian sloops, anchored all around us: such graceful, rippling booms and masts. (Evidently there are no straight trees in Haiti.) Many of their decks were piled high with fish traps and sacks of bottles. The boats were clearly trading as big a load as each could handle—and what was in that big pot that the Haitian woman was always stirring over the cooking fire on deck??

Sitting at a lovely historical spot called the "Queen's Staircase" one afternoon, we were interrupted by a small boy who came up to us and began a little speech about the Queen's Staircase (the history of...). He went so fast that I had to interrupt, at which point he had to go back to the beginning, like a spider spinning a web, because

Haitian
sloop

everything was memorized in sequence. Although we
didn't give him the quarter that he seemed to think it
merited, Chuck got him talking man-to-man about business and gave him a few tips, such as advising tourists
on the best angle from which to snap a good photograph
of the water. (A truly helpful piece of info from what we
could see of the passing tourists as they snapped their
photos.) We moved to another spot nearby to write post-
cards and looked up occasionally to see several small
boys running up to tourists and turning themselves on
like phonograph records, but only one was dragging
them off into the flowers to frame a more picturesque
shot of the falls.

Then onward to the Exumas, another lovely sail
through relatively shallow banks and deep bottomless
blue dotted with drifting (bright) yellow sargassum weed

and crystal white foam. I was all over the boat snapping pictures of water, sails and weeds, because it was all so lovely. Shafts of sunlight penetrated the depths. Undulating underwater sunbeams. Awesome! We passed over the Yellow Banks, which appeared as rows of reef and sand stretching from north to south like a furrowed field of alternating strips.

Our landfall at Norman Cay was, for a change, easy and uneventful. From this point began a series of day hops down the Exumas—Hawksbill Cay with its dazzling white beach, high green hills and rock cliffs; Staniel Cay with its little settlement where we spent a few days; Farmers Cay and George Town, Great Exuma.

Staniel Cay was a notable stop for several reasons. We anchored relatively near another boat, and soon we were conversing with its occupants about the odd tidal eddy current we both seemed to have anchored in the midst of. They invited us over for a visit that evening and, as is often the case, conversation got around to boat history and the background of our boat. After hearing our story of how *Alondra* had burned in a grass fire before Chuck bought her and rebuilt her, our host jumped up and yelled, "We have *your* stove!" And they did. After *Alondra* had been declared a loss by fire, Mystic Shipyard cleaned her up and sold most everything of value from her interior—including her stove, which was sold to the people we now sat with. There was no question about the stove's origins. It was a lovely little British model, a three-burner propane unit with a broiler-oven that exactly fit the oddly small space in our boat where no stove we found would fit.

Stoves have been a sore point in our lives ever since we began considering the problem back in Stonington. We simply could not find a stove to fit the space; all were too big. As we cruised down the Intra-coastal Waterway, we were measuring stoves as we went, and even now we are travelling with a standard-size, too large and thus un-gimbaled, Willis. We

will either have to shorten the Willis by cutting out a section and having it welded or remodel the galley a bit.

Fortunately, the pangs I felt at meeting *Alondra*'s original galley stove were not too great. Being a cook, I'm very attached to my galley, but we don't want a propane unit. What's fun is that—finally—the longstanding riddle of our stove has been answered once and for all.

Staniel Cay is also the place where we learned how to clean a conch. We were lucky to have been shown all the little tricks by a local Bahamian expert, because it's not as easy as it looks. In fact, there's quite a knack to "knocking" a conch. The edible part of a conch is the foot muscle, which is permanently attached to the inner spine of the shell. To remove this muscle without making a total mess of things, you must "knock" a hole at just the right spot on the spire, insert a flexible knife, and then peel the muscle off the shell by scraping with the knife from top to bottom. (The knife blade must be long enough to reach down the length of the shell.) When done correctly, the animal slides out easily. An expert can knock a conch in seconds with a quick flick of the wrist; the rest of us just struggle along at our own pace. Once the conch is free of its shell, it's time to "slop" it. The head, gut and entrails (collectively called the "slop") are cut away, leaving a slab of meat (called a "conch meat") that is white and fairly tender at one end, but extremely tough and covered with grayish skin at the other. What happens next in terms of preparation depends on the recipe, but it usu-

ally includes peeling off the grey skin followed by lots of pounding to tenderize the flesh. For knocking, slopping, peeling and pounding we use a hammer, chisel, fillet knife and mallet. With these trusty tools and some patience, we have been enjoying a variety of conch-based dishes. Conch salad (raw with lime juice, mayonnaise and Tabasco sauce) and conch Polynesian style (with pineapple, green pepper, soy sauce and ginger over rice) are particularly nice.

# The Simple Life
## *(or how to cope with no refrigeration)*

*ALONDRA* HAD NONE OF THE AMENITIES that most modern-day sailors take for granted. She had no inboard engine (we used a 9.5-hp outboard for navigating crowded anchorages). She had no electric lights in the cabin (we used an Aladdin lamp to read by). And she had no refrigerator. These omissions were by choice. When I met Chuck in 1972 (I was a student in his course, Underwater Research Techniques, at the University of Connecticut), he was rebuilding *Alondra* with a dream of sailing around the world. Chuck was very capable around engines and wiring, but he favored the simple life, which meant avoiding reliance on systems that were prone to breaking down and needing spare parts that were difficult to come by. Systems that we take for granted as being basic necessities on land can become sources of ongoing frustration and anxiety on a small cruising boat, especially if the system breaks down while out at sea or on a remote island. Self-reliance and peace of mind go hand in hand, and on a 28-foot sailboat, *less* is usually best.

While I loved the idea of simple self-sufficiency, I had zero experience in storing food and preparing meals on a boat in the tropics without refrigeration or an oven. Fortunately, I had some time to learn.

Our cruising journey began in Stonington, Connecticut, in November of 1973. Winter weather was already upon us, so

Flame tamers

keeping food chilled posed no immediate challenge. By contrast, learning to bake without an oven held immediate hands-on appeal, because my culinary adventures would keep the cabin warm. As we headed down the coast and along the Intracoastal Waterway, I gleaned knowledge from classic books, including Eric Hiscock's *Cruising Under Sail* and Helen and Scott Nearing's *Living the Good Life*, as well as soliciting advice from other cruising sailors, and soon I was filling our cabin with the warmth and fragrance of my cornbread and banana nut cake experiments. It took a bit of practice, but by the time I met *Alondra*'s original stove and oven unit face-to-face at Staniel Cay, I'd become proficient at baking pressure cooker sweet breads and skillet biscuits using one or two flame tamers. The one recipe staple I'd abandoned after moving on board was breakfast granola, which required a good toasting. No matter. Our new breakfast staples were hot oatmeal and fruit and grab-n-go skillet oatcakes. Yum.

By the time we reached a latitude where warming the galley with hot food took a back seat to keeping our produce cool, I'd already found answers to many of my questions. For example, overhead mesh hammocks proved to be much better places for

## *The Simple Life*

storing fresh fruits and vegetables than bins or ice chests. The soft mesh cushioned the produce from bruising due to rolling and banging, and it allowed us to see the produce easily. We could quickly spot those items that were ripe and needed eating, thereby minimizing rot and wastage. By comparison, a chest full of ice was messy and time consuming to maintain.

I learned that fresh eggs, kept protected and out of the sun, would keep for several weeks in warm climates without ice or refrigeration. (By "fresh" eggs, I mean those bought at local markets and not from large food chains, which rely on food transit systems and storage hubs.) Furthermore, the simple act of turning eggs upside down every two or three days helped extend their shelf life. Turning eggs helped keep the membrane inside the shell from drying out and becoming porous. Historically, voyaging sailors coated their eggs with lard, oil and (later on) Vaseline, which kept them fresh for many months. I tried this technique and quickly discovered how messy it was. Thankfully, we had no need to preserve eggs for many months because fresh eggs were available at most island markets.

Aside from storing eggs, keeping mayonnaise fresh had been my other big concern. Mayonnaise has such a reputation for causing food poisoning that I was surprised to learn that Hellmann's mayonnaise was safe to keep unrefrigerated, despite all warnings to the contrary. According to the cruising sailors who passed on this useful tip, this was because the pH of Hellmann's mayo was acidic enough to greatly retard bacterial growth, and the egg yolks in the recipe were pasteurized. Commercial mayonnaise brands, such as Hellmann's, should all have a safe pH level (4.0 or below). The rules to follow were simple:

1. Buy small jars that you can use up within a couple of weeks. (Remember, the ingredients can still go rancid, which leads to the next two rules.)
2. Keep your mayo away from light and excessive heat.
3. Discard your jar if the flavor seems "off."
4. Don't contaminate your supply by dipping dirty implements into the jar to remove mayonnaise.
5. Once you mix the mayonnaise with any other food (as in making egg or tuna salad sandwiches), the rules no longer apply. Once blended, don't allow your mayo-laced meal to sit around for long. Eat it promptly and discard any leftovers.

We followed the rules and we never had a problem.

Up to this point in our journey, we'd been sailing along the western side of the Exumas, so we were relatively sheltered from swell. It wasn't until we passed through Farmer's Cay Cut to the windward side of the islands that we began to have a bit more respect for such phrases as "slogging to windward." Windward sailing on a quiet bay or lake is one thing, but when seas are coming more or less head-on, they cut sailing speed dramatically. We spent all day making the 40-mile trip from Farmer's Cay to George Town, and since the harbor is not well marked by lights, we spent some more time tacking about offshore until the moon rose and we could see our way in.

Before going into town to top off supplies, we spent a relaxed day anchored off Stocking Island, enjoying the usual crystal-blue water rimmed by white-pink sand beaches and scrub-lined green hills. (Wearing polaroid glasses turns every view of a bay into at least 10 shades, from sapphire through turquoise to jade green.) We beachcombed and then snorkeled on the bit of reef that was nearby. And guess what! As Chuck dove down to set the anchor after our arrival (it's good practice to be sure the anchor is set snugly in sand), he found a surprise. Lying on the bottom, next to the anchor, was a mesh bag containing two sets of masks, fins and snorkels. The masks were fairly corroded, but I now have a new snorkel (a better model than my own) and, interestingly enough, one set of flippers fits Chuck and one fits me!

We picked up some fresh water and supplies at George Town—a pretty little town all in pastels—and on the following day we headed for Long Island (Cape Santa

Maria), where we were invited to cocktails at the Long Island Club by some older couples from Memphis. They were so intrigued by the opportunity to meet people off a cruising sailboat that they showered us with endless questions.

From Long Island, we intended to continue east to Rum Cay then down to Acklins, however it was now late in the season, fronts were few and far between, and we had agreed that if a front came we would ride it east, no matter where we were. The most difficult part of this passage to the Virgin Islands was the easting we would have to make to 69° latitude and 22° longitude before setting a course to Puerto Rico. A northeaster would theoretically carry us east for two or three days with winds behind us before returning to its usual blowing-in-the-face direction.

The weather had been unusually calm—the sea flat—on the way to Long Island, and it remained so through the evening when it appeared to be blowing out of the south. By dawn the wind was SSW, clearly some sort of front, and we decided that unless the wind (which was light) pooped out altogether, we would continue east past Rum Cay toward 69° 22°. For a change, there were three other boats anchored near us, and we all weighed anchor at approximately the same time, so we had sailing company for a while. We'd only met the occupant of one of the boats. He was a fifty-year-old man who was single-handing it from New York, bound for the Virgin Islands. His boat had no vane steerer (useful to self-steer a boat, especially at night, so a solo sailor can get some sleep without feeling the need to be at the helm 24 hours a day).

Upon rounding the point of Long Island, we began our first truly open ocean sailing that was unbuffered by any islands or banks. The sea was flat due to the light winds, but the ever-present ground swell was an amazing thing to watch. Unmasked by waves or chop, it appeared as great rolling hills of pastureland, behind which the other boats would rhythmically disappear and reappear.

There is nothing like being at sea for watching weather-cloud formations, shower zones and the puffy line of clouds on the horizon that means land will appear shortly below it. The line of rainsqualls that accompanies a front can be seen in plenty of time to don foul weather gear and close the hatches. Then the squall hits—*bam*, like a cloudburst—and for a short period, all visibility is shut down in walls of water. Then it's gone and every-thing is full of water. (Our cockpit is self-bailing, by the way.)

By dusk Rum Cay had disappeared behind us, but unfortunately so had the wind. The night watches (three hours on, three off) were peaceful except for the slat, slat, slatting of limp sails. The last thing we'd expected on this leg of our journey was doldrums-type weather! But here we were. We finally had to drop the mainsail

to ease wear and tear on our nerves, not to mention wear on the sail. Most of my watches I spent singing to myself—whole albums from beginning to end—which worked well for keeping me awake. There is something extremely peaceful, be it day or night, about being at sea in a small boat. Life becomes very simple, yet not dull, because every action has a purpose—of course, bad weather is something else again.

I had the early morning watch (4-7 a.m.). It's a tremendous experience to watch the stars fade. As dawn approaches, the clouds (always about 50-50 cloud cover) turn smoky, then peachy and finally the sun rises over a glassy sea. On this particular morning there was hardly a breath of wind, and as we clipped along at the great pace of perhaps one knot or less, I watched a couple of waterspouts snaking down from a brown cloud along the horizon. Suddenly, there was bird chatter nearby, and something that flashed in my mind as a "long-tailed tropicbird," though I'd never seen a live one, circled our boat trying to land on one of the spreaders. It was a beautiful

White-tailed tropicbird

white bird with black on its wings and two very long and slender tail feathers. Discouraged by repeatedly unsuccessful attempts to land on the fantastic piece of driftwood it had found, it eventually flew away. (Throughout the day we saw more of these lovely birds, and I wished for the umpteenth time that I had a bird guide with me.)

Still marveling to myself as the tropicbird flew off, I turned my gaze from sky to sea. And by golly if I didn't almost fall into the cockpit with new amazement, for right below me as I looked over the rail swam two of the most beautiful fish imaginable. In the morning light, there was no surface reflection to hamper vision through the crystal water, nor were there any ripples. These two dolphinfish were easily one-and-a-half feet long apiece. Their bodies were an intense sapphire blue with almost iridescent sky-blue spots on their heads and along the borders of their pectoral fins, while the tails were vivid chartreuse. They had evidently come to investigate the propeller of the outboard (mounted on the transom) as it spun idly in the water. After a few spellbinding moments, they finned lazily away. Glorious creatures!

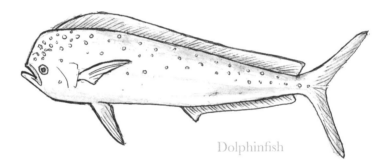

Dolphinfish

Throughout the day, the seas remained glassy to barely rippled, and we saw many dolphinfish (one-and-a-half to two-feet long) as they cruised about the boat near the surface. Most were flecked with bronze and gold, some greener, some bluer. They are supposed to be voracious feeders and easy to catch, so I dabbled my fingers in the water and one came near me to watch. He hung right by, so close with his mouth open, that I hastily withdrew my hand, not wishing to learn about "first aid at sea" any sooner than necessary.

The water remained smooth and unbroken all day, except for the little schools of flying fish and the great leaps and splashes of dolphinfish in hot pursuit. *Alondra* rolled along with the swell under jib and mizzen, while our sextant sights showed that we had made only about 50 miles.

By late afternoon a breeze suddenly appeared, and we began moving at a good pace under full sail in a matter of minutes. In a matter of hours, the sea had picked up quite a chop, and we began our second night in foul weather gear, etc. The nerve-wracking slatting had given way to anxiety-causing sounds of wind whistling through the rigging, the rush of water, and hard smacks of boat hull on wave.

Daybreak brought little change with the wind due NE, so often we had to go north or south of east to make any headway. Queasy and tired, we concentrated on eating and sleeping as much as we could.

The third night was worse than the last, with lightning and bits of rain, and a sea that by morning we estimated to be at least 15 feet and occasionally 25 feet high, averaging around 20 feet from trough to crest.

On the fourth day, we decided—for a variety of reasons—to head for the Turks and Caicos. Reason number one was that our bilge, rather suddenly, had to be pumped every three hours, and we wanted to determine the cause. Also, we were both worn out; not much of nutritious value had gone into either of us for the last few days, due to mental anxiety more than motion. (Eric Hiscock, whose books are the bibles of cruising sailors and who has circumnavigated the globe three times, discusses the adverse psychological effects of the sound of wind whistling in the rigging and waves smashing the boat—comforting to read, but it doesn't solve the problem.)

After taking a sextant sight and establishing ourselves as being directly north of the Turks and Caicos, we lashed the tiller (on a course heading NE, safely out to sea) and went below to rest, sip eggnog instant breakfast, munch chicken w/rice, and discuss our new insights about this business of being at sea and sailing to windward. We agreed that the days were fine, but night watches were awful without a third man to share watches at the helm, allowing for more sleep below. At 10 p.m. we began watches and turned SE towards, we presumed, the Caicos Islands. We figured on sighting land about dawn, and sure enough, at daybreak there on the horizon was a little dark smudge.

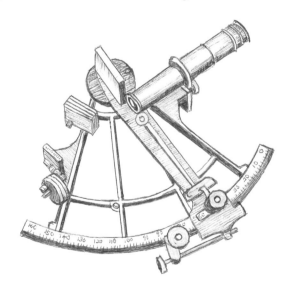

It took us all day to sail the length of the island—green, uninhabited, with white beaches and fringing reef. By 4 p.m., Chuck realized that either our compass was wrong or this wasn't the Caicos after all. (The Caicos and Mayaguana are remarkably similar on a map, except one reef runs south while the other runs southwest.) I took a sextant sight and, sure enough, we were at Mayaguana! We had not accounted for the strong northwesterly set in our dead reckoning. Nothing we could do now but anchor anyway.

We anchored on the southeast end of the island—completely uninhabited with a lovely sand beach, lowland with palms stretching inland toward hills, and a 10-mile long reef and lagoon off the east end. An osprey flew out to meet us, peeping and circling the mast, obviously delighted at having spied the tallest sitting post he'd seen in months I'm sure, and bent on making it his own. Every time the poor bird came in for a landing—legs outstretched, wings flailing—a swell would lurch the mast away until, in discouragement, he returned to his flat rocks and scrub.

During our earlier readings about sea passages, we had always wondered how everything gets wet inside the cabin during bad weather. Well, the point is that it does, and we soon had everything hung out to dry—so much so that the boat was all but hidden beneath mattresses, flapping sheets, towels and clothes.

We spent nearly a week on Mayaguana enjoying our own little island in the sun without seeing another

soul. There was so much to do! Beachcombing the white sand, we discovered glass fishing floats, some encrusted with glorious large purple barnacles and others with their netting still attached. We gathered beautiful little shells and pale purple urchin tests. We found the cast off carapaces of enormous land crabs, bleached to a porcelain white.

While exploring the rocky intertidal areas, we came upon tooth shells clustered together in cavities among the grey rocks, and black grapsid crabs that skittered away in every direction. The grey weathered rock itself contained coral and shells, including entire conch shells! How *old* were these shells? (Or, how young is this rock??) Conchs were everywhere on the bottom, and I had the chance to experiment with several new conch recipes for supper. Our fishing was a failure, however, because we didn't really apply ourselves to the task as we'd anticipated. In fact, we didn't find ourselves snorkeling that much, although we originally had high hopes of doing a lot of free diving in this isolated reef paradise.

On our first day ashore, we donned snorkel gear to have a quick look around from the beach, since it was already late in the day. As we entered the water, we were met by a myriad of fish and wavy green sea-grass. My first impression was, "Wow! I'm in Fairyland!" Almost immediately, Chuck tugged on my flipper, presumably to point out the school of big gleaming jacks that were racing past me to my left. I surfaced and nodded but instead he said, "Kathy, there's a five-foot shark in front of you." I have always wanted to see a live shark in nature, but I just said, "Oh," and made tracks for the beach. After all, it *was* late afternoon feeding time, and we *were* in a very remote place.

Lemon shark

So much for our introduction to Mayaguana diving! Chuck identified the shark from our books as a lemon shark; they're not an aggressive species, and none of the few attacks on record were fatal. Well then, we'll just snorkel earlier in the day when it's not their dinnertime. No problem. But then there was the three-foot barracuda who'd decided to take up residence below our boat. (I think he found the overhead shade of our hull to be very appealing.) Next morning, when I accidentally dropped a spatula overboard while washing dishes on deck, he zoomed in on it like a flash and followed it with his nose to the bottom. I allowed him full inspection rights before I went overboard to retrieve it.

This led to a little experimenting on my part. I took up my investigator's position in the dinghy and threw over a small line and sinker with a tampon that I had been wearing. Suddenly, there were three big barracudas all poking and mouthing the tasty morsel. I decided then and there that I would forgo diving until after my period.

The reefs were beautiful—covered with yellow and purple sea fans and other gorgonians that swayed gracefully in the currents. There were colorful varieties of Christmas tree, feather duster and other tubeworms, and more fish than we could imagine. We realized, however, that wherever there is a superabundance of fish, there will also be a healthy number of predators. That afternoon I counted nine barracudas hanging out below our boat, all between two- and three-feet long. Hmmm. We have turned out to be unabashedly chicken-hearted about diving in unknown, isolated areas.

Being thoroughly recovered from our "sea voyage," we decided to try again—after all, we had run into bad weather before, and had we stuck it out for a day longer, things would have improved. We decided to head to the Caicos (an overnight sail, according to our Bahamas guide), and if all was going well, we planned to just keep heading east en route to the Virgins.

This time the weather behaved well with a fair breeze and fair sea. Still, there was no getting around the fact that beating to windward in a small boat is a miserable task, even in fair weather. Our guidebook advised making an overnight sail towards the Caicos; at dawn, the eastern tip of East Caicos would be in sight, and a boat could come around it and shoot down to South Caicos. We left at noon to give ourselves extra time, but it wasn't until the following afternoon that we even sighted land. Not wishing to be too near land during darkness, we headed back out on an easterly course for the night.

The sea always seems to pick up at night. The wind screams in the rigging, the horizon and waves are invisible in the darkness, and waves continue to smash against the boat relentlessly. By morning, our nerves and stomachs were frazzled, and the waves were back up to at least 15 feet. A bit concerning was how often we found ourselves having to pump the bilge. Chuck suspected the constant battering by waves had worked one of the deck seams loose. (Not the teak itself, but the caulking between planks.) We agreed it would be good to haul the boat out somewhere and give her a thorough inspection. We planned to haul out "island style," by laying *Alondra* on her side and floating her up the beach on a high tide once we got to South Caicos. There, we could give the hull and decks a thorough inspection and do some re-caulking where necessary.

We spotted land again the next morning and headed around what appeared to be the eastern point of the chain. It took most of the day to run the 20-25 miles down to South Caicos. We were looking forward to a

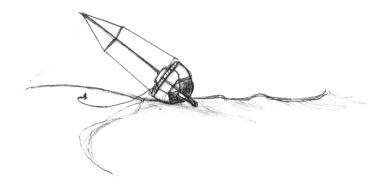

quiet night's sleep in the harbor, thankful that this time our cabin had remained dry and in good order. We talked idly about the patience involved in cruising, say, the Pacific, where charts are old and out of date and anchorages are unmarked and must be discovered by each voyager, often at the cost of a few extra nights at sea. "Take this island, for example," I said, pointing at the hills. "If this were unmapped (if there were no *Bahamas Guide*, for example, advising us to anchor at *x* and avoid *y*), we would probably be heading out to sea again to slog it out for another night."

These thoughts must have been my subconscious telling me that we weren't where we thought we were, for the very next moment, I realized that the coast we were travelling could by no stretch of the imagination be made to run south as it should towards South Caicos. We were, in fact, still somewhere along the north shore of the Caicos Islands, travelling southeast. So, now we were in that hypothetical Pacific position of not knowing precisely where we were along the unmarked shore.

Obviously, the safest place to spend the night in these circumstances is at sea, where there is nothing to run into or aground on. So out we went, tacking northeast and southeast every hour in order to remain relatively close to land. We adopted shifts of two hours on and two off, which was more satisfactory, but the night was rough, and everything got as wet as before! And we were pumping the bilge more often than before.

The discouraging thing about sailing east was that we were taking two steps forward and falling back one.

And on the northeast tack, we were getting set so far west that we made no easting at all.

We sighted land again by 8 a.m. the next morning and spotted what appeared to be the easternmost point of the Caicos Islands. Chuck decided that if it was not THE point this time, we would turn around, head west, and come around the inside of the islands. Fortunately, it was Drum Point (at the eastern tip of East Caicos), and once we rounded it, we had a glorious sail due south with a beam wind.

What a difference a direction makes! And what a welcome relief to be sailing on a beam reach instead of slogging to windward. We could actually get some things done that were not directly related to setting sails, steering a course or navigating. First, we set out a trolling line behind us to see if we could catch some fresh lunch. Almost immediately, we caught a huge gar-fish (needlefish) and cooked up a delicious stew of its sweet white meat with onions and potatoes. And of all things—it had blue-green bones!

I unearthed my carefully packed (and yes, still dry) collection of research papers that I'd gathered from the UConn library before our departure. I pulled out a paper called, "The Caicos Conch Trade," by Edwin Doran, Jr. I hadn't discovered this paper earlier, because it wasn't

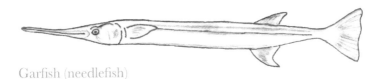

Garfish (needlefish)

about conch biology, per se. It was published in *Geo-graphical Review*, and it described an important trade of dried conch meat between Haiti and the Caicos, and its cultural ramifications. I sat in the cockpit and read it aloud, so both Chuck and I could learn more about the islands we were approaching and their relationship to conch. Because I'd designed my research proposal to answer the question of whether or not conchs migrate out of the protected waters of St. John National Park in the Virgins, I hadn't focused on fisheries issues elsewhere. As I read the article, I felt really lucky that our unscheduled, unplanned visit to South Caicos (thanks to bad weather and what proved to be a leaky deck seam) seemed to be leading us right into the heart of conch country.

As we neared the tip of South Caicos (Cockburn Harbour is on the southern side of the island), a new shade was added to the multitude of water hues we've seen—bright emerald green!

This letter is already way too long, so I'll cut to the chase. After I spoke with you on the phone to tell you of our whereabouts (by the way, I'm told the phone at the Admiral's Arms is the only phone in town), we successfully beached *Alondra* by careening her on the sand at high tide, located the leaky deck seam that Chuck had suspected, and mended it. In the 10 days since our arrival, we have connected with some wonderful people and, thanks to the many circumstances for which we take no credit, we seem to have ended up in the perfect spot at the perfect time.

Before I end the tale of our journey, I just want to say that this experience of sailing to windward has taught us why the trip east to the Virgins has the reputation of being such a toughie, particularly for small boats with a crew of two and no rotary vane steering gear (though wind-driven steering gear wouldn't have done much in the fickle winds we encountered). We have since met several boats with two and more crew, all experienced

sailors, who have adopted a "never-again" attitude towards long stretches of overnight eastward sailing (anything over one night or two, max). It can be done with lots of time, perseverance and discomfort, but we're not masochists. In hindsight, we're glad we've had this experience, though, because it shows that we can deal with assorted mishaps as they arise. I'm satisfied to realize how far I have come in my experience and abilities since those days back in Biscayne Bay—not to mention Stonington, Connecticut!

This seems like a good place to pause in this very long letter. I'll continue tomorrow, or as time permits.

*April 4, 1974*

*Continuing...*

### Why South Caicos

I had never heard of the Turks and Caicos Islands before discovering Doran's paper on the Caicos conch trade. They're a little British colony about 100 miles north of Haiti (you've probably found them on the map by now), as yet undeveloped by tourism, with many reefs and banks that are still unexplored. There are enormous salinas on the island with windmills left from the days when salt was a major export. Conch has been a major industry here for generations, with an average of two to three million "conch meats" being exported annually. We're told that the first internal combustion engine came to North Caicos just two years ago.

We played tourist for a couple of days in Cockburn Harbour before we began to entertain thoughts of staying. The town is a picturesque little place with pastel houses thrown together along clean dirt roads. I said "dirt," but the roads are mostly packed white limestone

sands and salt, with enough dirt in the mix to turn them creamy beige. Many roads are lined with low limestone rock walls. The overall effect is an almost dazzling brightness to the landscape during midday. Small children play happily with tin cans and sticks in the empty roads, and lots of pigs and chickens wander amiably about among the equally amiable dogs and cats.

At first appearances, it is judged to be a poor community, yet all the locals (called "Belongers") dress very well. We were told by several sources, "Don't let the locals fool you; they all have $10,000 savings in the bank and pay no taxes. They just put their money in different places—not in homes where there is no insurance when tropical storms occur and no water to quench a fire, but in clothing and travel. They dress very nicely and think nothing of popping off to the Bahamas, Miami, Dominican Republic and Haiti."

On one of our first strolls, we visited the enormous salinas that lie behind the town of Cockburn Harbour. There, we saw old windmills and sluices left from the days when there was an active salt industry here. Windmills pumped seawater into the salt pans where the sun evaporated it until the salt was ripe to harvest. We found a place called "the boiling hole," a natural underground connection to the sea that supplied saltwater to fill the salt pans. As we walked across the salinas, the late afternoon sun bathed the landscape in golden light, from the old rusted windmills (think warm brick-red) to the varied hues of the different salt pans (cream, white, beige and assorted pinkish-reds). Small patches of purslane accented the scene with splashes of chartreuse, which, combined with the pinks, made quite a spectacular scene.

As we walked slowly back towards the harbor and our boat, I noticed that the electrical poles running along the road were held upright with the help of support cables that had turnbuckles, just like the turnbuckles that tighten rigging on a sailboat. I suddenly wondered if all support cables bracing vertical poles used turnbuckles. Do they? Maybe I just haven't noticed until now.

Closer to the harbor, we came upon a huge pile of salt, greyish and crusted on parts of its outside, much like an old snowdrift. It sits in an open square behind the old salt loading dock. The salt mound stands taller than Chuck, and there's an excavation in it where townspeople come to take salt for their needs.

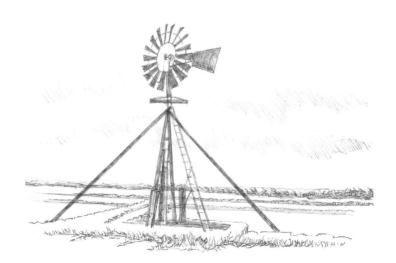

*A charming entrance invites our gaze.*    *Schoolgirls relax at the boiling hole.*

*Left: The scenic windward coast*

*Opposite page: A Haitian trading sloop moors at the old salt loading dock.*

Left: View overlooking the town of Cockburn Harbour. The District Commissioner's House touches the skyline, left of center.

Below: Hilly ("Cowboy") Seymour delivers drinking water to homes in town.

*Above: Townsfolk fill buckets of water from the government cistern in front of the Admiral's Arms.*

*Left: Lovely East Bay.*

*Below: Looking across the edge of town to the salinas (left of center).*

*Above: A large salt pile sits near the corner of Front Street and North Street.*

*Right: Friendly faces smile from a doorway.*

*Below: Children play along the harbor front near the old salt loading dock.*

We've met some of the locals—very friendly, hospitable people. Following the butchering of two sea turtles brought in by fishermen down near the slaughterhouse at Conch Ground, Lillian Jennings took me into her small house and taught me how to cook fresh turtle meat with native "peas and rice." Conch Ground is an area of waterfront where fishermen land and clean their catch. Conch meats are seen everywhere drying in the sun, pounded flat and strung up in rows like tan party flags on ship's rigging. Be careful if you stand downwind though...the powerful smell of drying conch meat is not for the faint of heart! I soon learned from Lillian that much of the conch I saw drying belonged to her husband, Julius. Aside from being friendly and outgoing, Julius also plays a mean ripsaw and leads a local band that plays at the Admiral's Arms on Saturday nights.

But back to turtles for a minute. While turtle meat isn't something I'd ever order on a menu in the States, turtles are commonly fished and eaten here, so I didn't pass up the opportunity to sample the meat of green and hawksbill turtles (both species are frequently caught here), as well as the eggs that were found inside the large green turtle. While the taste and texture of turtle eggs is nothing to write home about (except to say that turtle "egg whites" remain clear and jellylike, even after cooking!), turtle meat is quite delicious when cooked with a little onion, garlic, salt and pepper.

By our third day here we'd met quite a few people, and things began happening very fast. When I talked with you briefly, I mentioned that the Department of Fisheries was in favor of us staying here. Well, now I'll fill you in with a bit more detail.

The Admiral's Arms hotel is a central information hub for the town. Perched on a bluff, it's a breezy place to kick back and gaze out across Cockburn Harbour while catching up on the local news. Sailors, fishermen, visitors and locals all gather at the bar to drink (mostly Heineken beers out of green bottles) and swap stories with each other and the management. (Managers: Bart and Marianne Cotton from the U.S.; Assistant Manager: Tony Forest from the UK.) We've been coming here daily to grab ice-cold Cokes while taking breathers between bouts of working on the boat. (I say "here" because I'm writing you from the hotel porch overlooking the pool and entrance to the harbor.)

The bar is where I met Bob Parkinson. I was buying two cold Cokes to take back to Chuck at the boat when Bob and I began to chat. When I told him that Chuck was a licensed dive instructor and we were heading to the Virgin Islands where I planned to do field research on the queen conch, Bob jumped to his feet and exclaimed,

The Admiral's Arms

"You two have to stay here! Come tell this to the Fisheries Officer!" Not waiting for my reply, he took me by the elbow and off we went on foot, unopened Cokes in hand, to the Government Fisheries Building, a big white two-story house on the next hill over just a short walk from the Arms. The Fisheries Advisor, Tony Rae, was in, and when Bob told Tony that Chuck and I should stay in South Caicos so I could study Caicos conchs and Chuck could certify local divers, Tony was all for it. Still clutching two Cokes, I hurried to get Chuck and bring him over to Fisheries to get in on our conversation. And that's how it began...

Bob Parkinson and his wife, Chris, both 23 years old, came here about eight months ago from Ft. Lauderdale to run dive tours for the Admiral's Arms—special dive groups as well as tourists. They inherited a bunch of dive equipment and a few dive boats with instructions from West Indies Divers, Ltd. (aka WIDL), to make a go of it. Bob grew up in the Bahamas. He is an avid conservationist, and he also knows his way around boats and engines. He is eager for some assistance from Chuck because he isn't a certified dive instructor, and he won't take anyone out to dive that isn't already certified. There

Government Fisheries
Building

is a dive group coming in from the Midwest on the 7th, and Bob has invited Chuck to work with him on the tour to see how the operation works. There seems to be a good chance that Chuck can work with Bob, leading dive groups and teaching scuba diving to those who want to get certified.

We are keen on working up a collection of underwater slides to show to guests in the evenings, as well as introducing a bit of marine biology to the dive groups and perhaps eventually developing nature trips for students. Within a short distance are mangrove swamps, sandy banks and turtle grass communities, coral reefs, a "blue hole," bat caves, iguanas, etc., etc. Five minutes from the Arms is a terrific dive area called "The Wall," where the bank drops off from a depth of roughly 60 feet straight down to over 200 feet.

Bob and Chris took Chuck and me out yesterday to dive The Wall. (It's the name of a dive site, but "the wall" can also mean any underwater terrain that drops off steeply, forming walls of coral cliffs and ledges.) We went down to 110 feet and saw black coral (very rare), a patch of garden eels undulating upright in the current like a field of grass (à la Eugenie Clark), and many huge fish that were so unafraid of humans that we could almost touch them. In a word, it was spectacular.

Also, a couple of minutes from the Arms is a shallow snorkeling reef that is perfect for timid snorkelers and those who have never snorkeled before but would like to take a peek underwater at the beautiful fish and other coral reef life.

In case you can't tell, Chuck and I are really psyched about what the area has to offer for people interested in natural history. We would love to put together a little natural history booklet of the islands like the booklet that has been done on St. John, but realistically we'll probably never have time for that. I'm also anxious to do more painting, but I need a good set of watercolors—so MUCH to do here, and I haven't even begun to tell you about the conchs. But first I want to add, just so you know up front, that what the Arms *doesn't* have are swaying palm trees, sandy beaches, fine dining, or swimming and wading off the beach on a clean sandy

bottom…things you might hope to see when you eventually come to visit us.

So now, ABOUT CONCHS.

This is THE place to study conchs! The banks are
crammed with them, and the conch industry here is the
largest in the Caribbean region. As I mentioned above,
Tony Rae (his actual title is Turks and Caicos Fishery
Program Advisor) is very enthusiastic about helping
us stay here—all things educational are encouraged,
and no conch research has been done here yet. Given
conch's importance as a major industry and important
food source, the potential benefit to the local fisheries
and community here is exciting.

We have submitted a proposal to do conch research
here, and Chuck has applied for a work permit to teach
scuba diving and help lead dive groups. We are waiting
for the local government to respond. We have inquired
about housing, of which there is somewhat of a short-
age, so we may or may not get it. It is obvious to Chuck
and me that it will be challenging for us to live on a
28-foot sailboat anchored in the harbor all year without
fresh water for showers, while going diving every day
for my work and cleaning our equipment every day after
returning from the field. As far as I'm concerned, I think
having a refrigerator would be nice, too, if we should
happen to come across one with a house attached.

*Friday, April 5, 1974*

*Still working on this letter...*

Good news! Today we learned that our conch proposal has been approved, and Chuck has been granted a two-year work permit to earn some income. I am going to write a letter each to Dr. Towel and Dr. Rankin, and Chuck is going to write to Dave McCarthey, to tell them about our change of plans. On the following pages I am listing the reasons, more or less, that have made us decide to stay here in preference to going to St. John.

1.  In St. John, I would be working in 30-80 feet of water. The conch banks here are 0-35 feet deep; much safer, more time can be spent underwater, and a larger area can be covered. The banks are relatively protected from ocean chop, unlike St. John—again, safer and fewer days of non-surveying due to bad weather. Also, there is no crime here to speak of; very friendly people, and I can walk freely at night without concern.
2.  A paper written here would have relevant impact on the local industry. The Fisheries Department is enthusiastic and will be of aid, giving us use of their facilities—both office space and boats.
3.  Chuck may be able to work for income much more easily here than on St. John. He has already lined up a diving course and may be able to integrate well into the hotel's tourist trade. Here, he can work with me and also teach divers—no transportation problem here, and we don't have to be separated.

4. We will be able to catch occasional free hops to Miami on various planes. South Caicos is a stop-over point for planes flying to the islands and being delivered to Brazil, so planes are frequent, giving us access to the Miami area science libraries.

5. The local fishermen have spent generations of life-times fishing conch from the banks—their wealth of knowledge can and should be tapped.

6. I chose to study conch for its practical value as a fisheries and food resource. Here, we have an opportunity to work directly with the T&C Fisheries Dept., which I feel can add more immediate relevance and value to the community than working with a research station like VIERS or Island Resources Foundation.

But enough for now—time to send this off!

*All love, Kathy*

PS: Could you please send down the rest of our boxes to be mailed, but hold the box of clothes for now? (No need to get dressed up around here, and the boat's a bit too cramped for them.) Thanks. Send by air, or better yet, take over to Dave McCarthey's office on main floor of Life Sciences to be sent with the rest of my research material. Address: Kathy Orr c/o Mr. Tony Rae, Advisor Turks & Caicos Fisheries Dept., Cockburn Harbour, South Caicos, B.W.I.

*April 12, 1974*

*Dear Mom and Dad,*
It seems we've arrived at an excellent time. We've been given space with desks to work at on the ground floor of the Government Fisheries Building, a wonderful two-story complex overlooking the harbor. Richard Stevens, a British VSO (Volunteer Service Overseas) in his early twenties, is here on a two-year term to do some lobster research. He and Tony Rae have been setting up a wet lab with running fresh and salt water. There is a huge concrete seawater tank in a screened-in porch adjacent to our workspace where Richard will be doing research on spiny lobsters, and the surrounding floors will be tiled next week. The Fisheries Office itself is upstairs, and Tony Rae and his family live in the spacious residence that adjoins the two-story Fisheries complex. How exciting to be in "on the ground floor" of this budding new lab, figuratively and literally! Chuck and I are enthused by the opportunity we have to do some useful work here.

The islands are being discovered quickly. It seems that every plane brings in new schemers and developers. In the last week or so, 200 acres were sold on South Caicos alone. Chuck says South Caicos reminds him of a California gold town just before the big boom. Primitive and lovely with delightful people. He says he's almost afraid to go to sleep at night for fear he'll awaken and find it all gone—covered with concrete and neon lights.

Which reminds me...before my memories of first impressions disappear beneath the crush of new events to write home about, I want to take a moment to describe a couple of my favorite scenes from the harbor. There, some of the older fishermen still gather conchs from the bay using a glass-bottom bucket and a long pole. The fisherman sculls along in his wooden skiff using a single oar to maneuver the boat. Periodically, he uses the glass-bottom bucket to look below the water surface and view the bottom. When he sees a conch, he sends down the

long pole with his free hand and snags the conch off the bottom using the bent, fork-like tines at the end of the pole. Then, hand over hand, he pulls up the pole and flips the conch into his boat. Obviously this method is depth-limited, but fishermen tell us that conchs used to be so plentiful in the shallow waters around South Caicos that they would actually walk up onto the beach and be exposed at low tide.

Conchs "walking" may sound funny, but it's an apt term, because they don't glide like other snails. Using their powerful foot, they heave their heavy shell forward in the direction they want to go, and then step up to it, then heave the shell forward again and step up to it again. (Think of a one-legged man on crutches and you'll get the gist; throw crutches and weight forward, then step in, and repeat.)

I also particularly love the sight of the graceful island-style sloops with wide bellies and long booms, like the Haitian sloops we saw in the Bahamas. Many have dried conch hanging in the rigging.

We visited some of the processing plants the other day and watched women process conch meats and also spiny lobsters (the locals call them "crawfish"). I got to see tails of the other three lobster species that grow large enough to harvest, although they are much less plentiful than spiny lobsters. Spotted lobsters and slipper lobsters I'm familiar with, but I got to see my first smooth-tailed lobster, the least common of the four.

Scale fishing is quite a big trade here as well as conch and lobster—frozen fish is shipped all over, including large amounts to the Virgin Islands. I learned that most fish eaten in the Virgin Islands is imported due to the prevalence of ciguatera (fish poisoning) in those waters, so the fish you eat on the menu listed as "native snapper" in the Virgins is more than likely a frozen import—perhaps grouper from the Caicos!

*Love, Kathy*

# Ciguatera: Reef-Fish Poisoning
*Before you eat your catch,*
*gather local knowledge.*

I LEARNED OF CIGUATERA (pronounced sig-wa-té-ra) shortly after Chuck and I arrived in South Caicos. We were cleaning the day's catch of fish down by the harbor when a local fisherman approached.

"You planning to eat those?" he asked, pointing to two lovely jacks we'd caught just an hour before. "Maybe they make you plenty sick," he said, looking at the sky. I told him I had eaten some the previous week with no ill effects, but asked him what he meant. He said there were certain fish no one ate because they were poisonous and could make a person very ill. He explained that different fish were poisonous on different islands, or even different parts of the same island group. He shrugged as if to say eating the jacks was a gamble we could choose to take, or not.

We didn't eat the jacks, and we considered ourselves lucky to have been warned early. During the two years we lived on South Caicos, we met many cruising sailors who had been stricken with ciguatera, a form of seafood poisoning caused by eating certain tropical reef fish. We heard chilling tales of intense itching for weeks, of hair falling out, of a couple so weak they could barely lift their limbs to crawl on deck and wave to a nearby yacht for help. A local friend told us his grandfather had died of ciguatera after eating barracuda.

Those were the severe cases. It is likely that many minor cases of ciguatera go undiagnosed and unreported every year, being confused with other forms of food poisoning.

Why is it important to know about ciguatera? Because there is no easy way to identify a toxic fish before eating it; because the toxin is stored within the body indefinitely; because there is no known antidote; because ciguatera is an ongoing part of the lives of many tropical island cultures today, continuing to affect their social and economic patterns as it has done throughout history.

Symptoms of ciguatera poisoning are inconsistent and diverse. They may vary somewhat from person to person, from region to region and with the species of toxic fish eaten. The chief indicator symptoms of ciguatera are exhaustion and weakness; intense itching; tingling, numbness or burning lips, hands and feet, and a sensation reversal of hot and cold. This last symptom, where ice cream feels tingling hot and steaming coffee feels cold, is surely the most bizarre and telltale symptom of all.

Symptoms may appear immediately or up to 30 hours following ingestion. Gastrointestinal symptoms, including nausea, vomiting and diarrhea, may be experienced for the first day or two. Other possible symptoms include slowed pulse, lowered blood pressure, headaches, painful joints, incoordination, blurred vision and increased light sensitivity of the eyes. In severe cases, loss of hair and nails, blindness, convulsions and coma can occur, and in a small percentage of cases, death occurs due to respiratory failure. The duration of symptoms depends on the amount of toxin ingested, the victim's age, physical condition and whether he or she has had ciguatera before. Duration may be measured in days, weeks or even months.

## *Ciguatera*

There is no immunity. Instead, subsequent poisonings are increasingly severe because the toxin is stored in the body. This explains why two people can eat the same fish and one may become ill, the other not. Often sensitization occurs where ingestion of any fish or alcoholic beverage will trigger a mild recurrence of symptoms. For this reason, some victims of ciguatera stop eating fish altogether.

There is presently no antidote to ciguatera poisoning. Standard initial treatment is to induce vomiting or have the stomach pumped to remove as much of the toxic source as possible from the body. Following this, a variety of treatments have been used to combat symptoms and alleviate physical stress. These include B-complex and C vitamins, calcium gluconate, magnesium sulfate, aspirin, cortisone, mannitol, oxygen when breathing is impaired, and cool showers to relieve itching.

Toxin-bearing and non-toxic fish are indistinguishable to the common senses. They look, smell and taste alike. Consequently, folklore has developed around methods of poison identification. Claims that a copper penny turns green or a silver spoon tarnishes when boiled with a toxic fish, or that flies and ants will avoid toxic fish, are not grounded in fact. There are only three ways to know if a fish is toxic: eat it, feed it to another animal and watch for signs of illness, or send a sample to a lab for testing. Unfortunately, there is no way to detoxify a toxic fish. The poison survives boiling, baking, broiling, freezing, pickling and drying.

Ciguatera occurs throughout the tropics and subtropics of the world in areas associated with coral reefs, but some areas are more severely afflicted than others, and the areas where toxic fish are caught are patchy and can change over time. In general, ciguatera outbreaks in the Pacific are most prevalent among the eastern Pacific islands such as Tahiti, while in the Atlantic, the Virgin Islands are the main hot spot. Beyond this, the characteristics of when and where ciguatera occurs read like pieces of a puzzle. Toxic fish are found abundantly in some islands but are totally absent from others. Around an island, toxic fish may prevail in certain areas that change over time, increasing, diminishing, disappearing and appearing anew somewhere else. Sometimes the areas where toxic fish occur show seasonal patterns, sometimes not.

In terms of fish species, the occurrence of ciguatera is equally unpredictable.

Some fish within a species may be toxic while others are not (even around the same island), and different fish species may be commonly toxic in different islands. Even symptoms of the illness can vary from region to region.

Given these characteristics of its occurrence, in 1958, marine biologist Dr. John Randall hypothesized that fish were consuming a toxic marine microbe of some kind as they fed on plants and scavenged along the bottom. As predatory fish consumed these herbivorous and scavenging fish, the toxin was passed from fish to fish throughout the food web.

Nineteen years later, Randall's theory was confirmed. In 1977, researchers in Hawaii isolated the toxin (ciguatoxin) and researchers in Japan traced the toxin to a marine dinoflagellate, a tiny single-celled plant-like organism. *Gambierdiscus toxicus*, named for the Gambier Islands where it was discovered, grows in shallow water areas associated with coral reefs. (Researchers subsequently isolated additional toxins made by *G. toxicus*, including maitotoxin, which explains why symptoms of ciguatera vary from region to region.)

## *Ciguatera*

Since then, researchers around the world have been working on ways to identify toxic fish without the need for its consumption. The radioimmunoassay (RIA) can measure the toxicity of fish tissues directly using radioactive isotopes. An

1. A microscopic organism called *Gambierdiscus toxicus* produces a poison called ciguatoxin.

2. *Gambierdiscus* thrives on algae in certain locations, under certain conditions at certain times.

3. As herbivorous fish consume contaminated algae, they ingest the toxin and store it.

4. As carnivorous fish consume herbivorous fish, the toxin is passed to them, and on up the food chain.

5. As people consume toxic fish they consume the toxin and store it. When the toxic load becomes high enough, a person develops symptoms.

enzyme-linked immuno-sorbent assay (ELISA) and a receptor-binding assay (RBA) have been devised that use substances that change color in the presence of ciguatoxin. Although field test kits based on these methods have been developed for research purposes, an inexpensive test kit does not yet exist for individual use.

Growth of *G. toxicus* has been linked to disturbed environments, such as dredged harbors and dead coral reefs. As human activity has increasingly disrupted coastal environments, ciguatera outbreaks have become more common and widespread. Today, ciguatera is the most commonly reported form of seafood poisoning.

Occasionally, ciguatera outbreaks occur when toxic fish is delivered to markets or restaurants and sold or served to many unsuspecting consumers. But because there are regulations outlawing sale of known toxic species in most islands, these sources are normally safe, and most visitors to the tropics can spend their vacations oblivious to the problem. Local knowledge is usually enough to protect those who catch their own food, provided they know to seek it out.

Some 400 species of reef fish have been implicated worldwide in ciguatera outbreaks. Given the pressures that climate change, overfishing, marine pollution and marine habitat degradation have placed on marine species, it is increasingly common for people to choose to reduce or avoid consuming reef fish. Ciguatera risk is just one of those reasons. A general rule of thumb is that predatory fish "high on the food web"—such as barracuda, amberjack and the green moray, as well as older, larger fish—are more likely to have concentrated the toxin than smaller fish. By following these simple precautions, people can prevent ciguatera poisoning:

## *Ciguatera*

1.  Limit or avoid consumption of reef fish.
2.  Do not eat the brain, spinal cord, intestines, liver or roe of reef fish, because ciguatoxin accumulates in these organs.
3.  Never eat barracuda, moray eel or other "high risk" species of fish.
4.  If you plan to go fishing for your own consumption, seek local advice first.

If symptoms appear after consuming a fish, contact a physician immediately for treatment, and avoid eating reef fishes for at least three months after all symptoms have disappeared. If possible, write down the following information and report it to your local health authorities (along with a tissue sample of the fish, if you have it): your symptoms, the name of the species you ate, the size of the fish you ate, and the location, time and date of capture.

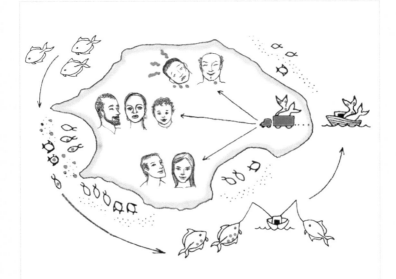

Today, ciguatera is the most common form of marine fish poisoning worldwide, and yet relatively few people know about it. This is because the specifics of this form of poisoning read like the pages of a good murder mystery. The toxin goes undetected by our five senses. The first warning sign is usually when someone gets sick. Because the illness is a function of toxin accumulation, two people can eat the same fish, but only one person might fall ill. And two fish of the same species might be caught in the same place at the same time, but only one fish might be toxic. Ciguatera poisoning does not originate within the fish itself, but from the habits and feeding patterns of the fish during its lifetime. This means the site of the toxic algae might be nowhere near where the fish was caught. And where the fish was caught might be nowhere near where the fish was consumed.

*April 22, 1974*

*Dear Mom and Dad,*

Before I forget, would you please share whatever parts of my letters you think would interest Chris (I'm sure you're doing that already) and then send them along to Alison so I don't need to repeat myself? Thanks. I find I have little time to write and no time to journal, so these letters will serve as a record of my time here, haphazard though they may be.

Chuck and I have just returned from a plane trip around the islands—sort of a quicky sight-seeing trip with Paul Loughrey, one of our friends who works for Ray Morgan flying cargo around the Turks and Caicos and to Miami, Nassau and Haiti. Paul had some extra room between the grits and the frozen chickens, so he took us along to North Caicos where he dropped off the supplies at Bottle Creek Airport. Bottle Creek Airport is a little dirt airstrip in the middle of scrub cactus with a small blue house at the end. We flew over the town of Bottle Creek as we came in, buzzing low to let the townsfolk know we were arriving so they could drive out to the plane and pick up their supplies. Then we flew on to Providenciales ("Provo") following along the northern coast, and then back to South Caicos flying over the Caicos Bank. From the air, it is immediately apparent how much of the Caicos is actually a vast network of tidal rivers, salt pans and flats studded with dwarf mangroves and laced with tidal creeks, reminiscent of a scorched counterpart to the Everglades. Roads and settlements are all but non-existent on the bank side of the islands.

By contrast, the seaward side of the archipelago (the islands are all really part of the same plateau, separated by narrow channels) is higher and greener, with more pine and palm trees. Along almost the entire north coast runs a wide white strip of beaches with blue and green lagoons, beyond which lies a fringing barrier reef and scattered coral heads—looks like there's fantastic virgin diving along all of these shores! On the southern side of the islands, the Caicos Bank seems to stretch on forever in all directions—potentially fine conch grounds and nursery areas for marine life.

We have become quite settled in and feel more a part of the community here. The locals are warm and welcoming, and there is more for us to do here than we will ever have time for. At least we'll never die of boredom—fatigue and heat prostration maybe, but not boredom!

The dive group came and went with great success (how can you miss with novice divers from Nebraska!), and it was an interesting experience for me to see how the managing end of a dive group works (Bob and Chuck mainly). I really enjoyed diving with the people and explaining a bit about the reef community they were seeing—pointing out various forms of marine life and animal behaviors, etc. The visitors seem to see more and enjoy it more when they learn something about what they're looking at. Maybe we'll be able to work out a seminar program at some point that will cater to groups interested in learning about the various marine environments. There are certainly enough knowledge-able people here, as well as potential facilities available. In the one-and-a-half to two years we plan to be here for my research project, perhaps we'll work something out.

I picked up my watercolors again, but not in the way I'd like to imagine—no leisurely moments spent con-templating a scenic vista. Rather, I was working for a cause. One of the divers in the Nebraska group, a nice fellow we'd befriended, found a live cowry snail during a night snorkel. Despite Bob and Chuck's policy of "look but don't touch," he couldn't resist bringing the snail back to the hotel, hoping to enlist some kitchen help in the morning to clean out the shell so he could take it home as a souvenir. This morning, Chuck suggested I go over to the Arms and try to coax our friend into giving up the cowry. Well, the moment I saw it, I immediately understood his passion to keep it. The snail was gliding around in a jar of seawater—a gorgeous Atlantic deer cowry with a four-inch long shell. Its ultra-glossy shell (rich chocolate with creamy white spots) was perfect; it was truly a prize. Oh dear. I chatted for a while about the thrill of collecting being in the discovery of a new speci-men, not in the killing and keeping of its remains, but our friend wasn't swayed. Then it struck me that I could paint a "portrait" of the cowry that he could hang on his wall as a memory of his find and a story to tell his kids. I offered to make a painting of the cowry in exchange for its life, and he agreed. I'm glad to report that the story ended happily, with a lovely painting and big smiles all around, and one very lucky cowry that was returned to its home.

Atlantic deer cowry

Last week Mr. and Mrs. Armour of Armour Star Meats were here for two nights at the Arms, ending a four-week vacation in which they went island hopping around the Caribbean in their private plane. Since part of Chuck's role is now to help Bob find guests who want to snorkel, scuba dive or go fishing, he invited the Armours to go snorkeling. We took them to a shallow reef, where Mrs. Armour began her explorations by charging smack into the Elkhorn coral like a runaway train. Oh dear. Fortunately, she and the coral both survived, and things improved from there. The Armours turned out to be avid nature enthusiasts who were amazed by all they saw. They invited us to dinner, but since we had a previous engagement (no, our social life isn't always that busy), we had some rum punches with them at the bar and told them about our ideas for bringing in nature groups to learn and appreciate the natural world here. They loved the idea so much that they gave us their card, asking us to keep in touch and let them know if we wanted any "assistance." Next morning, they approached Chuck and asked, "Would it help you any if you *owned* West Indies Divers?" (Were they actually offering to buy it for us??) We said no, but it was a very kind offer.

We are presently house, dog- and cat-sitting for Bob and Chris, who have gone to the States for 10 days. Living in a house is a welcome treat, but we discovered that roosters in South Caicos don't begin to crow at dawn; they start near 3 a.m. (Our theory is that South Caicos roosters are the same as roosters everywhere, but elsewhere, the ones that begin to crow in earnest before dawn get butchered pretty quickly.) No word on the status of our own house yet, but tonight we're going to dinner at Richard's (the VSO student working at Fisheries). An ex-pat who deals with government housing will be there, so we expect to learn something.

Meanwhile, I am anxiously awaiting word from Dr. Rankin or Dave McCarthey about whether they'll allow me to do my research here. In anticipation of their approval, I plan to continue scouting out conch areas for study—I simply can't imagine there would be any problem with me working out of the Caicos instead of St. John.

*Love, Kathy*

*May 8, 1974*

**Dear Mom and Dad,**

Last Friday Christy, one of the conch fishermen, took Chuck and me on a tour of the nearby conch beds so we could evaluate the best spot at which to carry out my research. Christy says we can "find conch most every-where," but in summer there are more conch in shallow waters. We visited four different habitats, including the padina flats (*Padina* is a kind of seaweed) between Mid-Six Reef and Six Hill Cays. All the conchs we saw at this site, even the adults, were smaller than the norm. (While this size discrepancy is worthy of study, it makes the padina flats a poor site for my project.) The other three sites were off Six Hill Cays. Six Hills is a good distance from South Caicos, but it's the best location for my purposes due to its distance; the conch fishermen only rarely go there to fish.

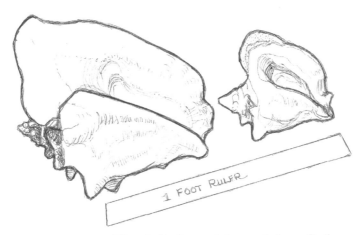

The shell of an adult conch from *Padina* flats is much smaller than the norm.

One of the Six Hill sites was a mix of shallow patch reef and sand off the southern end of Long Cay. Christy says that this is where conchs "come out of the sand." Several fishermen have told us there's a "conch mine" in this area. They say conchs emerge from the mine full grown to walk the bottom where they can be fished. When fishermen take the ones walking on the bottom, new conchs emerge from the mine to take their place. Some fishermen have a different theory. They speculate that conchs "levitate from the deep" and reach the Caicos plateau in that fashion. The fishermen do have some very creative ideas, but they're also interested in learning more about conch and protecting the industry.

*Friday, May 10, 1974*

**Dear Mom and Dad,**

I received a letter from Dr. Rankin today saying that I should by all means go ahead with my research project. Yay!

I also got a letter from Alison saying she'd like to visit this summer, if possible, and I am encouraging her to do so—can't wait! We haven't adventured in nature together in years. Should be fun!!

On top of all that, we received news that the government can supply us with a two-bedroom house by the end of the month. So, with some luck, Alison will have her own bedroom to sleep in. There are motorbikes to ride all over the island, sunfishes to sail, beaches on nearby cays to have all to one's self, snorkeling and diving galore, not to mention a conch project to help with. It's great that Alison's into diving—I think she'll love all the things there are to see and explore here.

Of course you are all always welcome to come visit, too! But regarding a visit on the way or way back from St. John, you've probably discovered that the Maine phrase, "You can't get theah from heah," applies rather well to the Caicos. Mackey Airlines flies to and from Miami every Tuesday, Thursday, and Sunday, and that's it.

News-wise, we're bustling as usual, although hustling and bustling goes on more slowly here because of the hot climate.

My conch studies are coming along fine. I've been field-testing survey methods for tracking conchs and testing underwater tag designs to see what works best.

I've been eager to get an idea of how far conchs might move on a daily basis, so I tagged a bunch in a shallow grass bed right in front of the Fisheries Office. When I checked on them the next day, I was amazed that one had "walked" approximately 150 feet overnight!

Meanwhile, West Indies Divers is getting ready to receive another group, and Chuck is finishing up teaching his dive class. How fortunate we are to have a Coast Guard LORAN station at the north end of the island. It supplies Chuck with a steady stream of young guys eager to learn to scuba dive, and it also has a ditto machine that we can use to run off tests and teaching materials for the dive students.

Tonight there is a party at the Coast Guard station and our friend, Julius Jennings, will be there with his island band. Every time we turn around, there seems to be a birthday party or some other happening to go to. Chuck was chuckling just this morning about how active our social life became after we arrived in South Caicos.

There are so many things from clothes to books that I wish were at my fingertips, but they aren't worth asking you to send. I have got a request though…it seems I'm good for at least one request a letter. I hope you don't mind, but it's the way things are done here. Locals and residents who need items that aren't available on island send requests to their family members who live in Nassau or the States—the items are mailed by family members, or they're brought back by anyone making an outbound flight. Such items are: most clothes, film, sunglasses, sneakers and most shoes and sandals, hand mirrors, stationery, unavailable food items—actually, nearly *everything* except what you might pick up in a small corner drugstore that acts as a five and dime and grocery store rolled into one. Anyway, my request today is to you, Mom. Whenever you are in a clothes store, would you please pick up a little summer shift or two? The weather is extremely hot, and since I'm essentially living in bathing suits beneath my clothes, something light and easy to slip on and off would be perfect. Thanks.

*Love, Kathy*

*June 8, 1974*

*Dear Mom & Dad,*

How delightful to receive your letter and hear that you are planning to visit! I have reserved a double room for you at the Admiral's Arms. We think it would be great if Chris wants to stay with us (providing we have a house by then). We *should* have a two-bedroom house in town by the middle of this month. June seems to be one of the more rainy months (most are completely rainless) so maybe our little island will be in a more greenish mood when you get here. As I reminded Alison—you can't buy film here at the hotel, so be sure to bring all the supplies you want with you when you come. Looking forward to seeing you all!

On the conch front, I finished my pilot studies, and we're now working on plans to set up a big underwater grid off Lower Six Hill Cay. I plan to tag the conch within its central squares and then follow their movements over the course of one year. I'll also be noting their growth and behavior (and whatever else seems pertinent) throughout the study. Six Hill Cays seems to be an ideal study site for tracking conch movements in that it's far enough from human contact to stay relatively undisturbed by local fishermen, it's sheltered by the nearby cay so anchoring the dive skiff is easy, and the water depth is only 12 to 15 feet, so we have unlimited dive time, which is a huge plus when making field observations. It's interesting to note that both Six Hill Cays were formed from piles of empty conch shells tossed there by humans across a span of countless years. Over time, they have turned into small islands covered mostly with a mix of purslane and other very low vegetation.

Recently I went on my first night dive with Chuck and some Coast Guard friends that he had certified. We dove in the harbor and shallow reef areas. How amazing to be underwater at night! Ctenophores and comb jellies in the water column around us shimmered with iridescence when we touched them. I found a basket star whose unfurled arms completely transformed it from the ugly wad it appears to be by day into a thing of amazing delicacy and beauty as it feeds by night. We saw parrotfish sleeping in their mucus cocoons and goatfish wearing their nocturnal colors. I even learned how a coral crab manages to dine on living *Diadema* (long-spined black sea urchin) as I quietly watched from behind a coral

rock. Well, I won't let myself get started on the list of what we saw, because there is so much I would want to describe. Some of the fish change color at night, displaying patterns and stripes that they don't show during the day, and many small creatures like arrow crabs and cowries are out and about. There's a kind of sea cucumber that extends its front end from the shelter of a stony crevice to feed at night. Its long, slender form looks like a necklace of translucent baubles. At one point, I got a big surprise when I shone my dive light beneath a coral head and peered inside. As quick as a flash, big green cheeks and a gaping toothy mouth lunged right against the glass of my facemask! I had unwittingly disturbed a fat green moray eel. I don't know which one of us was more startled and alarmed, but he was clearly telling me, "Get outta my space!" Of course, I was happy to oblige.

*June 19, 1974*

**Dear Mom and Dad,**

Today we got the keys to our new house! It's an island-style house in town. Perfect location within walking distance of everywhere we need to go. I'll try to keep this letter short because you'll be here to visit soon enough, but here's a quick rundown just so you get the gist. The house is stucco with corrugated metal roof and a big yard to one side. (Well, I should say, "as seen from the road." The front of the house actually faces the yard, not the road.) One enters the main room via a wide screened-in porch. The main room has a sitting area in front and a metal kitchen table and fridge in the rear. A small single-bed guestroom opens to the right, and the kitchen, master bedroom and bathroom are all to the left. The kitchen has a gas cooktop and oven, and there's a small open shelf with gas broiler above the cooktop—never seen that before, but it looks really handy.

Outside the screen door that exits from the kitchen is a water catchment under a separate roof. A large metal lever enables us to hand-pump water from the cistern up to a gravity feed water tank on the roof. This water feeds our kitchen and shower, while the toilet uses saltwater. Stanley, who gave us the keys, apologized for the fact that we don't have an electric water pump to fill our gravity-feed system. Well, no need for apologies. After all the manual bilge pumping we've done while cruising, this will be a piece of cake, not to mention the fact that when the electricity goes out in town (which it does), we can always pump water. Despite plenty of dust (the house

abuts the road and the trades make everything dusty) and floors with sheets of ripped linoleum throughout, we're very pleased with and grateful for our new abode!

Other events have been less cheerful of late. Namely, Bob and Chris Parkinson haven't been paid in months for their work with West Indies Divers, Ltd. (WIDL). There seems to be something fishy afoot with the company and cast of characters that hired them. Porter and Lindsey (two of WIDL's shareholders) were in town earlier, but Mr. Triester (another WIDL shareholder) has been the Parkinson's main liaison. He flies out here from the mainland at roughly two-week intervals, but he's been bringing Bob & Chris bags full of groceries instead of a paycheck. We've been cat-and-house sitting for Bob and Chris while they're away on the mainland hoping to sort this out.

*Love, Kathy*

*July 3, 1974*

**Dear Mom and Dad,**

Well, the latest surprising news is that Mr. Triester told Bob that he and Butch Moody (another WIDL shareholder) have bought West Indies Divers! They want Bob and Chris to continue working for them, but there's really no way Bob and Chris can ever work for those two. Bob and Chris are among the few who really understand what a natural treasure these waters have to offer, and they're as passionate as we are about working to conserve these fantastic marine resources for future generations. These values, alas, are all too rare, and virtually diametrically opposed to Triester's and Moody's plans for the dive operation moving forward.

Now on to conch…

Last week, a group of us made a run down to Six Hill Cays in the *Watchful*, the new Fisheries patrol boat, captained by Turton, who works for Fisheries. Turton dropped off Chuck and me with our gear and the Fisheries skiff boat, then took Richard and some others a bit farther south to check on Richard's lobster traps. Chuck's and my project that day was to map the population density of conchs along Lower Six Hill Cay in order to plan the placement of the conch survey grid. Our method was to swim a series of underwater transects running perpendicular to the cay, with Chuck swimming a compass course in the lead as he unspooled a measured line and me following the line with a wide horizontal rod, counting and recording all conchs visible in its path.

Running the series of transects went well enough, but we had something of a standoff with a big barracuda who tried to tell us that this was *his* territory, not ours. The weather was grey and overcast, which lent a general feeling of gloom to the underwater scene. Add to this the unwanted attentions of this big fish (I presume he singled me out for his territorial displays because I'm smaller than Chuck), and it was one of the spookier dives I've done. Chuck and I carry spears from our Hawaiian slings for purposes of communication underwater—we tap the metal spear shaft against our tank when we want to get each other's attention—but today I felt grateful just to have a spear in hand, for psychological reasons more than anything else. We'll see how we get on with him as time goes by. With a bit of luck he may not stick around.

*Love, Kathy*

*July 28, 1974*

**Dear Mom and Dad,**

Yesterday we actually had a lazy morning; what a treat! I'm reading Steinbeck's *East of Eden*, and Chuck is reading Kerouwac's *On the Road*. We packed a picnic lunch along with our books and rode our bikes to the graveyard. (Did I tell you we inherited two bikes from Paul Loughrey? He got a new job as a pilot for Turks and Caicos Airway—good news for him but sad news for us, as he had to move his home base to Grand Turk.) At the graveyard, we found heaps and mounds of cups and plates on some graves. We read peacefully under the pine trees and then headed down to the old customs dock for a swim. We found Bob sitting at the dock. He told us he and Chris will be leaving for the States on Tuesday's Mackey flight. He said it's a temporary move, but long enough for them to make some money. They are giving up their house here. We will miss them, and we hope, as they do, that they'll be back here before long. Nevertheless, it sounded pretty permanent to me.

We decided to pack a supper picnic and ride out to the salinas, but once we got there we chose to just keep going. We biked up to the Coast Guard LORAN station and arrived in time for the movie, *Distant Trumpet*, with Troy Donahue and Suzanne Pleshette. It was a finky western, but somehow appealingly corny.

Today we picnicked out at Highlands with Hugh (Hutchings), Paul (architect from Bermuda), Mooney, Beverly and her cousin, Alex Reid, Mike Ritchie, and Bob

Highlands

and Chris. It turned into a goodbye party for Parkinsons. We will all miss them a lot.

Gotta close now. Tomorrow there's a big State Council meeting up at the Department of Fisheries to discuss the processing plants vs. co-ops and Haitian employment. We'll also be helping Bob and Chris pack up to leave on Tuesday.

*Love, Kathy*

*August 17, 1974*

**Dear Mom and Dad,**

Just to set the record straight, Bob Triester and Butch Moody did *not* buy WIDL after all; that turned out to be just another of Triester's "tall tales" (we've dubbed him "Tricky Triester"). Without going into the draining details of this particular drama, it suffices to say that the tangled plot is worthy of a season on soap TV. (The plot would run something like this: A group of shady characters go in on a business deal together. As long as they only use and abuse *other* people, they survive as a team. But when they start turning on each other, chaos ensues.) Apparently, Mr. Waterworth (another shareholder) now owns WIDL outright, and Triester and Moody are out. With each shareholder telling us a different story, though, it's hard to know what's really true. The main thing is that WIDL's mission is now to run high volume back-to-back dive groups. Bill Waterworth (Mr. Waterworth's son) ran the dive operation before the Parkinsons took over from him (Bob Parkinson says Bill Waterworth didn't like the job), and now Bill has returned to run the dive operation once again. Poor Bart and Marianne have been holding rooms at the Admiral's Arms for multiple dive groups promised by Triester, none of which have materialized. They've been looking at their empty hotel feeling increasingly stressed out, so I do hope things settle down soon. Bill Waterworth seems to be as unenthusiastic about running WIDL as Bob said he was, so I suspect his father must truly be the owner. Otherwise, Bill's return would make no sense.

Hugh Hutchings, Mike Round ("Skipper" at the base) and Al Reid all dropped by separately to talk today. Hugh stayed until afternoon, talking about people leaving, about island people and attitudes, and what "could" be done but hasn't been. Hugh will be leaving for Europe at the end of the year. Sorry to see him go. We agreed that so often it seems that the less ethical people with "balls of brass" get away with murder, so to speak, because those who are more ethical are unwilling to go through the mucky process of holding them accountable.

Case in point, I'd been hoping that Richard, the young VSO who has been here for almost two years studying lobsters for the fishery, would become a friend and colleague on the marine research front. But Richard doesn't seem to know biology from the back of his hand, and he doesn't seem to care, either. He's a good-natured "bloke" who uses his gift for being a natural comedian to charm his way out of one tangle after another. He allowed me to read his annual report before sending it off to England. The report describes his study as being an investigation of spiny lobster growth and survival on an exclusive diet of conch slop. ("Slop" is conch entrails that are discarded while processing the meat.) The question of how to convert useless waste into helpful food for mariculture is certainly worthy of study. But the reality of this "study performed under laboratory conditions" is that a bunch of neglected, starving lobsters are being held in the big tank at the fisheries lab along with lots of other marine animals, and nothing about the tank, its occupants or their feeding is being monitored. In general, they are surviving by eating each other. (I saw one desperate lobster grabbing at a live fish!) When I said, "Richard, you know as well as I do that those lobsters are eating everything BUT conch slop!" Richard lifted his eyebrows, looked at me with big, sad, puppy dog eyes, and said that he had no funds with which to BUY conch slop to feed the lobsters (State Council withheld his last $2,000 check… guess why), so therefore he was powerless. (Of course a visit to the processing plant just down the road would give him all the slop he could possibly want.)

There was more in the report. It mentioned reef transplanting efforts and the monitoring of coral growth in the laboratory. (Aha! Could this be what that one dead lump of Elkhorn coral that's been sitting in the lobster tank is supposed to represent?) This is just the tip of the iceberg here; there's a lot more I won't bother to go into. I will say, though, that as I watch Chuck reading Richard's report, I think I see steam beginning to blow from his ears…

*Love, Kathy*

*August 21, 1974*

**Dear Mom and Dad,**

Lately we've been coming up here to Fisheries after supper because it's easier to get more work done when people aren't always dropping in to chat. But one never knows who will drop by, or when. Last night, Dyke Stubbs stopped by and told us stories until 9 p.m. Dyke's a retired lawyer who usually wears a white shirt and long black pants that seem to enhance his head of flowing white hair. He loves to kick back in his chair, a bottle of spirits in hand, and tell lively stories from his early life. And we love listening! He's got an amazing blend of knowledge and lore tucked away in his mind, and you just never know what gems he'll bring forth. Tonight, he entertained us with a story about "educated bedbugs" and another story about a bottomless well. He said there's a bush in the mountains of Haiti that has a scent that keeps you sleeping, and another bush that has the antidote. He also told us there's a single "flying feather" on a chicken, and without that single feather, the chicken cannot fly up into a tree.

*August 25, 1974*

*Continuing...*

When Chuck and I aren't building the survey grid or diving (or recovering from a long day of both), we like to go beach combing. We sometimes walk to East Bay and Shark Bay to see what the waves have washed ashore. It's funny how my eyes and Chuck's are drawn to notice different objects. Chuck's attention zeros in on things like square corners because he's keen on human artifacts and signs of human history. I'm interested in natural history, so my eyes select for organic shapes instead. I love finding sea beans, including "horse eyes" and "sea hearts," which Hugh Hutchings says drift here from the mouth of the Amazon River.

Occasionally, we come upon a glass fishing float. Maybe the reason I love these particular human artifacts so much is because they remind me of glassy bubbles and they're colored like the sea. We've found several of them along these beaches, all from four to six inches across, in pale shades of aqua, green and lavender. One

of my two favorites, which I found on Mayaguana, is a four-inch green glass ball that sports the empty shell of a giant purple barnacle. My other favorite is my latest acquisition, which comes with a story attached…

Last week, Mike Round invited us to accompany him in the Coast Guard skiff to Long Beach for a relaxing day of beach combing and snorkeling. Long Beach runs for miles along the windward coast. It is as beautiful as it is remote, and we never know what treasures we'll find there.

On this particular day, there was no wind and the ocean was glassy calm. As the three of us walked along the sands of Long Beach, Chuck and Mike were deep in conversation. My eyes were scanning the sky and sea, appreciating the day, when I spied a small speck on the otherwise flat horizon. It was far up ahead and far out at sea. I kept my eye on it as we walked, and over the course of the next half hour, I could tell that it was coming closer to shore, slowly drifting in from the open ocean. I began to suspect it was a large glass ball (the kind used by fishermen to hold up their nets), neither as big nor as far away as I'd first imagined. I trotted ahead of Chuck and Mike, eager to confirm its identity and wanting to meet it, whatever it was, when it finally made landfall. I kept walking, the object kept drifting, and when our two trajectories finally converged, I waded into knee-deep water and plucked it from the shallows before it hit the sand. It was a beautiful, turquoise glass ball, a foot across, still in its netting, and dripping with live gooseneck barnacles on its underside. The discovery of a large glass ball along the beach would feel special in itself, because these balls are so rare. But to stand in the shallows with open arms and receive such a gift upon its arrival felt altogether awesome! Where had it come from? How far had it journeyed? Who'd held it last, and for how long had it drifted? Perhaps to some folks this event would seem small, but for me it was right up there on a par with picking up the perfect plough anchor for *Alondra* while crossing the Bahama Banks, out of sight of land.

*Love, Kathy*

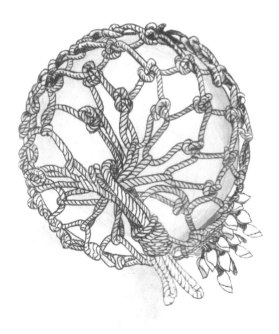

*Right: Locally built sloops among the mangroves.*

*Left: A policeman making his rounds strolls past Dyke Stubbs's old law, turtle, and sponge office.*

Left: A tailor's shop along St. George Street at the intersection of Graham Street. We passed it almost daily on our walks from home to our boat and the Arms.

Opposite page: Far left: An old windmill, once used to pump seawater for making salt, still stands amid the salt pans.

Left: Boys play ball in front of St. George's Anglican Church.

Above: Chuck and Dyke Stubbs enjoying a chat in Dyke's yard.

Left: Porch at the Admiral's Arms.

*Beach combing along remote shores near the Coast Guard LORAN station.*

*Below: Impounded Haitian sloop tied to the government dock. (One of three sloops that were confiscated for smuggling marijuana, found stuffed inside radiators.)*

Above: The local ferry, Caicos Joy, transported people and goods among the islands.
Below: View from the Admiral's Arms. Two cannons from an old shipwreck "guard" the harbor.

Below: The government house provided to us for our work. The cistern (far left) collected water, which was pumped to roof level and flowed by gravity to the bathroom and kitchen. The red roof covered a screened-in porch. North Street is on the right.

*September 3, 1974*

**Dear Mom and Dad,**
I wrote a long letter to Dr. Rankin to bring him abreast of my research progress thus far. I'll sum it up for you here, while it's fresh on my mind:

"CONCHS WALK PLENTY!"

Which is to say, they move a lot farther and faster than I anticipated.

I think I mentioned the tagging experiments I ran on a handful of conchs in the grass bed just off the Fisheries building back in May. I used a simple survey method—a circular search pattern using measured nylon line and compass to determine distance and bearing of conchs from my point of release. I made daily surveys to measure the distance they covered every 24 hours. It became quickly apparent that conchs are more mobile than I had expected! Those conchs moved an average of 52 feet per day, and some moved roughly 120 feet per day.

A second pilot test followed in which we built a small version of the grid we've now been setting up at Lower Six Hill Cay, and we tested the methods we will be using in the official study over the next year. Using items in abundance on the island—ballast rocks, lobster buoys, netting and lines—our pilot grid had 16 buoys arranged in four rows of four, with 30 feet between each buoy, making a 90 x 90-foot grid overall. I tagged 20 conchs in place on the bottom to mimic the tagging procedure of the official study. It seems clear that two-part tags are the best way to go, with the ID number staying close to the conch, while the replaceable float makes for easy visibility. We used clipboards with underwater paper and pencil to plot the position of each tagged conch within the grid. Then back at the lab, I transferred each conch's position onto its own individual spreadsheet to develop a picture of how each conch moved over the duration of the pilot study. It didn't take long for the adult conchs to move out of the pilot grid. Two months later, one of those tagged conchs was picked up by a tourist while diving in East Bay—in a spot over a mile away from the grid.

It seems clear that conchs move much more extensively than J. Randall noted in his studies on St. John. I am beginning to understand the local fishermen's claim that they can fish a large area clean of conchs, return in two to three weeks, and find thousands more! Of course, there are many factors influencing conch movements. One of these is age. The conchs I tagged were a mixed group of adults and large "rollers" (juvenile conch that have not yet formed a flared lip). While the full-lipped adults moved extensively, every roller moved only a foot or two per day. I will be monitoring environmental

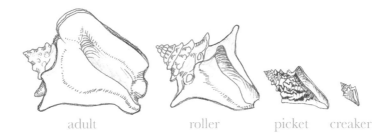

adult          roller          picket    creaker

conditions throughout the study's duration to see what patterns emerge relative to weather, season, etc. Aside from the particulars of my project, I am curious about all aspects of conch behavior and will be keeping copious notes. Chuck and I have not yet found any baby conchs ("creakers") less than 5 cm long. They must be here somewhere…lots of mysteries yet to unravel!

*Love, Kathy*

*September 18, 1974*

**Dear Mom and Dad,**

The days go by so fast! We are slowly, slowly cleaning up the house, which is still full of lots of odds and ends left from Bob and Chris's departure. We inherited the lovely round grass mat they brought back from Haiti, as well as a set of Haitian wooden plates and bowls. I thought the mat would be perfect for our living room, but the darkly patterned linoleum detracts from the mat's own lovely pattern, so we've placed it on the cement floor of our porch instead.

Chris left me with a bolt of sailboat-patterned material that she used to sew café curtains for their windows. I've been using it to make café curtains for our windows, too. The trade winds blow dust from the roads inside the house. It settles in a thin, pale layer over all surfaces pretty quickly, and café curtains help curb this accumulation.

I had enough fabric left over to make myself a sundress, so I dismantled my worn-out shift and used it as a template to stitch myself a new one by hand. Sitting peacefully in a chair doing needlework is a fun change of pace that seems to balance the heavy legwork of swimming transects underwater at Six Hills. It feels so "dainty" compared to sewing sails, though! Fortunately, I haven't had to sew any torn sails yet, but my typical "sewing gear" includes waxed twine, sail needles, and my left-handed leather sailor's palm, which I use to sew canvas and other heavy-duty items for the boat. I finally finished the set of blue sail covers I've been sewing for *Alondra*.

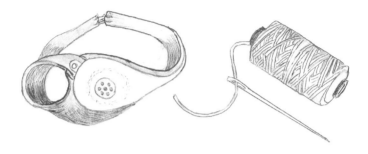

One project leads to another, and while we were in cleaning mode, Chuck and I pulled up the ripped sheet linoleum in our kitchen and also in the bathroom. I painted the cement floors of both rooms a misty grey-blue. It looks great! Of course, dusty footprints from our bare feet are always gathering, but we keep our trusty rope sailor's mop by the kitchen back door, and I just swish away the prints with a damp mop from time to time. (When it reaches the point where I begin to swish the paint away, I'll just do some touch-up painting.)

Oh, I forgot to tell you that Bob gave us custody of their old yellow Jeep. It has lots of idiosyncrasies, including a hand-crank starter that serves as back up for the key ignition system. When the Parkinsons were here, we used it to transport dive tanks and outboard engines. We continue to use it for that purpose, and thankfully Chuck manages to keep it running, as well as the outboard engines, "bearded wonder" that he is.

*Love, Kathy*

*October 7, 1974*

**Dear Mom and Dad,**

Both the Fisheries skiff boat and patrol boat (*Watchful*) have been out of commission, awaiting new engine parts from the States, so we decided to try taking our inflatable Zodiac to the study site. With two dive tanks apiece, two sets of dive gear, two full gas tanks, an anchor and us, it took us one-and-a-half hours to travel each way, but we got in a good day's work, nonetheless. We found only 53 out of the original 212 tagged conchs. I've already made a second batch of tags, and I'm currently planning to tag on a monthly or bi-monthly basis. The conchs seem to be moving eastward along Six Hills.

Our visit with Chuck's parents and sister was lovely, but short—a chance to catch a breather and take a quick tramp in the woods before heading to Florida to see Bob and Chris and take care of our long list of errands. We gathered needed supplies, including a bunch of reference books, texts and articles I wanted from Rosensteil School of Marine and Atmospheric Science and the Institute for the Oceans and Fisheries Library. Then we packed up and dropped our *200 pounds* of excess baggage at Miami Air Freight to send to South Caicos.

On Tuesday morning, we were at the ticket counter preparing to buy our return tickets when the seller asked our destination. I said South Caicos, and he replied, "Oh, we don't fly there anymore." (Huh??) "The airport burned," he said. (!) He knew no more than this, so we

boarded Mackey Airline, planning to get off at Grand
Turk and take Turks and Caicos Airway over to South
Caicos.

It turned out he was wrong, for we did land in South
Caicos after all. But from the scenery, it could have
been Middle or North Caicos, because the whole terminal building had vanished so completely that it took
me several minutes to decide where it had once stood.
Three flags and a few browned flower bushes were all
that showed the spot; not even rubble remained. Nearby
stood a little refreshment stand and a trailer housing
customs and ticket sales. (Too bad we never thought
to photograph the airport, and now it's gone.) Now I
have to write regular letters instead of sending cards,
because the island's only postcard supply went up in
smoke. But the island lost a lot more than postcards—
all the Caicos Company records and business papers
burned (the airport was owned and leased by the C.C.,
not the government), thousands of dollars in equipment
(much of it privately owned by the tower operator), Norman's office and contents, Dora's refreshments counter
and contents, etc., etc. An unfortunate discovery after
the fire was that the airport was not insured. We heard
that Bob Porter, one of WIDL's original five shareholders, had quietly let the insurance lapse and has since
tried (equally quietly) to slink out of the South Caicos
picture altogether.

The fire was thought to be the work of an arsonist,
though causes and culprit(s) will never be known for
sure. There are five rumored causes, but the most popular rumor among the locals is that the airport was burned

out of envy over Dora's new all-night food-drinks and music center, which opened not long before the blaze (Dora ran the airport snack bar). Rumor has it that some of the bar owners in town felt her new business was taking away their old customers. Of course, given all the records and business papers that went up in smoke, there could have been other motives at work. We don't know what's true.

*Love, Kathy*

*Above: I'm "knocking" a conch to remove it from the shell. Next steps are to clean the meat, squeeze on some lime juice, and enjoy eating it raw.*

*Below: A group of juvenile conchs nestle among seagrasses and algae at the Six Hill study site.*

*Right: Four of us head out in the Coast Guard skiff to dive the reefs.*

*Below: Preparing to set up a 100m² reference grid at the study site.*

*Left: Measuring conch growth.*

*Below: Conch shells on the beach: The shell lips identify them as an adolescent (upper left), a young adult (upper right), and two juveniles (below).*

Above: A healthy stand of elkhorn coral.

Left: Sisters suiting up for a dive. I'm on the left; Alison is on the right.

Below: Exploring a crevice along The Wall.

*Above and below: Diving on Tucker's Reef.*

*October 12, 1974*

**Dear Mom and Dad,**

Guess what arrived today—the lost box of vitamins and health foods! What a nice surprise. Other than stale cereal, things seem in quite good shape. Hopefully the missing field thermometers will follow.

We've been down to Six Hills twice more in the past five days. Both times we found approximately 70 conchs and have taken our second set of growth measurements. It's exciting to start compiling growth data. One of the tagged conchs buried itself in the sand and has remained dormant for five days. Yesterday, we found a second buried conch.

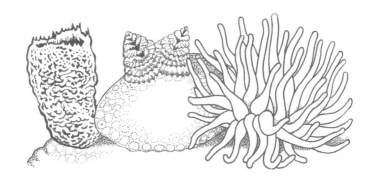

Jim Nolte, the leader of the first dive group Chuck worked with after we arrived in South Caicos, is down here for three weeks or so on a photography assignment. He is planning to make several collections of slides for Bill Waterworth, who has been running WIDL since Bob and Chris left. Jim's a great guy, and we've been taking him to lots of new dive spots—a great excuse to explore new places. He supplies the boat (from WIDL) and we are his guides and underwater models. Bill Waterworth really doesn't like to dive, so everybody's happy.

Saw a deep-blue Christmas tree worm on yellow-green star coral beside a lavender vase sponge; what a technicolor combo!

*Love, Kathy*

*October 17, 1974*

*Continued...*

Sorry this letter has been sitting around for so long. My problem is not in writing letters as much as in getting them sent!

In answer to your question, on a typical "Six Hills day," we do two dives (two scuba tanks of air) per trip; one tank before lunch and one tank after. Our lunch is usually homemade lobster or fish salad sandwiches with celery and tomatoes made on the bread baked by Mike Ritchie's mom. We eat them in the boat while discussing the morning's work. (We eat at least two very fat sandwiches apiece—we burn up lots of calories doing this work!)

Snaggletooth, our resident barracuda, is with us always at the study site. He comes and goes during our dives, and I am finally to the point of ignoring his presence. Now that he's no longer a problem, I don't mind telling you that those first few dives we did after we "invaded" his territory last July were really quite scary! At the time, I was hoping he was just a transitory resident. He didn't want us on his turf, so he tried earnestly to chase us away by putting on some very fierce and threatening displays. I think because Chuck is considerably larger than I am, he chose me for his target. Barracudas are normally silver in color and rather torpedo-shaped. But when they want to look fierce (think of a growling, snarling dog) they arch their backs, suck in their gut, raise their dorsal fin and turn a sooty grey color while wagging their head from side to side and snapping their jaws. Snaggletooth would do all this while rushing at me, head on. This is not a fun thing to experience. The first time it happened, I could only sit there hoping it was a bluff, and that he would veer at the last moment. He did. Nevertheless, he repeated this performance more than once.

He'd move away from me almost to the limits of visibility before turning and zooming like a missile directly at me. He successfully chased me back into the Boston whaler several times before we both learned to just relax and go about our business.

Once he got over his fear of us, Snaggletooth became quite curious. He now follows us around quite benignly. Nevertheless, barracudas have quick reflexes and they're often attracted to glinting objects and splashing, so we are careful by habit. Upon arriving at the study site and anchoring the whaler, we throw our dive equipment and clipboards overboard first and let Snag check them out. (He often goes nose-to-nose with the clipboard as it sinks…something about that white paper; maybe it looks like white fish flesh.) Then once Snag has satisfied his curiosity, we enter the water and

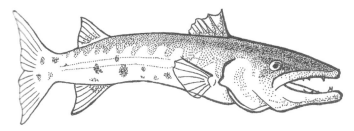

Angry barracuda

don our tanks and gear as we're sitting on the bottom. By now Snag knows we're not a threat, and he clearly loves to hang in the shadow of our anchored boat.

*Love, Kathy*

*October 27, 1974*

**Dear Mom and Dad,**

The seas have been really rough lately, but finally the weather is beginning to settle. Last Tuesday, while food shopping, I stopped by Lillian's store and picked up some of her "panny cakes" (sesame seeds from Haiti that are toasted in brown sugar). Then I stopped at Mooney's store to pick up some fresh eggs. While chatting about the weather, Mooney looked at her calendar and noted that tomorrow (Wednesday) would be the full moon. She said, based on this, the wind should keep blowing throughout the week. She said the first lunar quarter is never windy like this. The winds come around full moon, and when it's blowing this hard before the full moon, either rain will follow, or it will blow for four or five days. Well, of course I had to keep track of what happened… It blew hard through Thursday and a bit less hard on Friday as frequent showers set in, then more showers on Saturday, and today, Sunday, it's been drizzling all day. So Mooney's almanac gets five stars, and I'm using the rainy day to read, relax, bake pineapple brunch cake and catch up on writing letters.

In other bits of news, I recently gave a talk about the conch's life cycle to a group of fishermen. I was pleased and relieved to see how interested in and receptive they were to what I had to say. I think they believe what I tell them because what I describe rings true to their own experience and matches what they've seen. When I described mating conchs and mentioned that conch semen is electric blue, as seen when decoupling

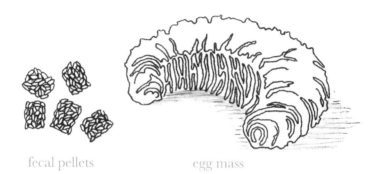

fecal pellets                    egg mass

a mating pair, there was visible enthusiasm and surprise in the room, because they knew I wasn't making this stuff up; I surely must have seen it for myself, as had they. When I described conch poop, they recognized those clumps of tiny pellets instantly and were interested to learn that the pellets were feces, not eggs— because those pellets *do* look like packets of tiny eggs.

Another piece of conch anatomy the fishermen were especially interested in was the crystalline style. It's part of a conch's digestive system, and it looks like a long translucent noodle. Our friend, Mike Ritchie (around 17 years old), has told us some hilarious stories about himself and his friends fighting over who gets to eat this prized gelatinous "noodle," because it's rumored to enhance a young man's sexual stamina.

*Love, Kathy*

*November 1, 1974*

*Dear Mom and Dad,*

We had two cruising sailors over for dinner last night. Fritz and Bill are both single-handers (meaning they cruise alone in their own boats), but the two are good friends, having recently spent a month together in the Bahamas. Due to an unforeseen accident at sea, they will now be spending more time together in South Caicos, where Bill plans to help Fritz make repairs on his boat.

When Fritz arrived in Cockburn Harbour two days ago, his 40-foot Alden ketch was leaking and in shambles. Both masts were broken, and the deck was covered in a great tangle of splintered wood and rigging. We learned that the ketch, while out at sea, had been struck by a passing freighter. The incapacitated boat had then drifted for more than four days before a U.S. Coast Guard cutter from Puerto Rico took Fritz aboard and towed his ketch to the dock at Cockburn Harbour. Over dinner, Fritz described his run-in with the freighter.

On the day of the accident, the weather at sea was fair with a clear horizon all around, so Fritz went below to fix himself a quick meal. He was inside the cabin when he heard a sudden rushing sound—like a ship bearing down on him—followed quickly by a terrible CRUNCH as his boat suddenly lurched and rolled. The freighter must have been going at full speed when it sideswiped his sailboat, pulling down both masts and rigging. Apparently oblivious to what had occurred, the freighter continued blindly on its course at a full clip, and soon disappeared over the horizon. Fritz said the freighter must have been travelling on autopilot with no one on the bridge to spot his 40-foot ketch.

Ironically, Chuck and I had just finished reading an interesting article in a cruising and travel magazine; it was authored by a man named Fritz, who had spent over 15 years cruising the Atlantic and Pacific aboard his lovely 40-foot Alden ketch, *Tumbleweed*. Now here was *Tumbleweed*, a floating shipwreck tied up at the dock, and here was Fritz at our table, a mass of scrapes and bruises, and lucky to be alive. Bill, who was en route to the Antilles, now plans to stay on in South Caicos long enough to help Fritz make his boat seaworthy enough to limp back to Florida. Fritz plans to work in Florida until he has earned enough money to rebuild *Tumbleweed* properly. It will likely be a long road, but Fritz just grins and says, "Well, at least I'll get an exciting article out of the experience. I think I'll call it, '*Sagebrush* Rescues *Tumbleweed*'. *Sagebrush* was the name of the Coast Guard cutter that towed the drifting *Tumbleweed* to South Caicos.

*Love, Kathy*

*November 20, 1974*

**Dear Mom and Dad,**

I only have time for a note today—been SUPER busy these days.

Conch project is going well. We have a couple of Coast Guard volunteers, Paul Roell and Joe Shepro, who are enthusiastic scuba divers and love to help us in the field whenever they can. They come to Six Hills with us in the whaler and help us with transects and sweep searches. It was funny to watch Snaggletooth checking them out. Snaggletooth recognizes Chuck and me, and he knows our routine by now, so he generally hangs beneath the boat while we work underwater. When we bring strangers with us, though, he likes to inspect them closely.

Tomorrow Chuck, Skipper (Mike Round) and I are going on an adventure to visit the Conch Bar Caves in Middle Caicos. Mike has finished his tour of duty at the Coast Guard LORAN station and will be leaving the islands in a few days.

*Love, Kathy*

# The Great Hammerhead Shark

FROM TIME TO TIME, those who go scuba diving along "the edge of the deep" report spectacular sightings of big ocean-going species, such as sailfish and tuna. Tony Forest, who used to dive with West Indies Divers, recalled the thrill of sighting a humpback whale one winter as he was diving along the edge of the drop off at a place called "The Wall," where the Caicos Islands plateau meets the deep waters of the Turks Islands Passage.

In 1974, the subject of several spectacular sightings was a 19-foot-long great hammerhead shark. On several occasions, he was seen cruising outside the harbor along the plateau between Dove Cay and the edge of the drop off. I can say the shark was 19 feet long with some confidence, because Bob and Chris Parkinson had the dubious pleasure of eyeballing him from stem to stern as he swam directly underneath the West Indies Divers 19-foot dive skiff (which they were in at the time). Male great hammerheads are known to reach 20 feet in length.

After that first encounter, Bob and Chris saw this shark twice more. The second time they saw him they were diving in the same area, 60 feet down, swimming along the bottom near the edge of The Wall. They were exploring a line of coral heads when the great hammerhead swam right past them. They didn't see him coming because he approached them from behind, and although he passed right next to them, he ignored them both and just kept going. "He passed us at eye level," Bob exclaimed. "It was like a submarine going by!"

"I swear his dorsal fin was six feet tall!" Chris added. "When I saw him I just froze, and my eyes filled with tears."

The third time Bob and Chris saw the great hammerhead shark, Chuck and I were diving with them, along with our friends, Paul Roel and Joe Shepro, from the LORAN base. All six of us were together on the flat area at 60-foot depth near the edge of the drop off when the hammerhead swam directly overhead. According to Chuck, the shark looked "like a 747" as it zoomed along about 40 feet above us. I didn't see the shark because, at that moment, I was thrilled to be getting a *very* close look at a gigantic green turtle that seemed quite unafraid of us. I was marveling at how she just sat on the bottom, motionless,

### The Great Hammerhead Shark

and allowed me to swim right up to her! Then Chuck pulled
on my flipper and waved me back to the boat.

By the time Chuck and I climbed aboard the dive skiff,
the other four divers were already on board, babbling excitedly

about a gigantic hammerhead shark. Shark? *What* shark? I soon realized the turtle I'd been watching had seen the shark, too, and *that* was why she had allowed me to get so close to her without moving. Paul said when he saw the shark, his jaw clamped down so hard on the mouthpiece of his regulator that by the time he returned to the boat, he'd bitten it almost in two. He held up his regulator and showed us the broken rubber.

Evidently, I was the only one of the six of us who had *not* seen the great hammerhead. Part of me thinks, *What an opportunity missed!* And part of me thinks that perhaps it was just as well.

*November 24, 1974*

**Dear Mom & Dad,**

Another note to say thanks very much for sending *Watership Down* and *All Things Bright and Beautiful*. I have just sneaked previews of them both, since I'm still reading another book, but I suspect I will really enjoy them.

I love having the time to read a lot—probably because there are no other diversions (i.e., TV and movies). I am now finishing *This Timeless Moment*, written by Mrs. Aldous Huxley (Laura Archer) about her husband shortly after his death. Both were remarkable people.

Chuck, Mike Round and I had a fun trip to Middle Caicos, where we visited the limestone caves and stayed the night. Middle Caicos is a step back in time where there's no electricity, no phones and people go to sleep when the sun goes down.

The Conch Bar Caves are extensive and of tourist quality. We were assigned a local guide, but often he just

Leota's house, Conch Bar

sat patiently while we probed various passages on our own. We brought plenty of lights (our diving lights), and in some parts of the caves we waded hip deep through seawater. In one little room, the ceiling was so low I kept bumping my head on small stalactites. We found no ancient artifacts, but we encountered plenty of bats!

Caves are definitely things that are greatly enhanced by proper and extensive lighting for impressive effects, but we gladly swapped that in our minds for the adventure of imagining we could perhaps be "first" to visit some spots. Not many people visit Conch Bar Caves, and those who do probably don't bring good lights or go exploring beyond where the guide takes them.

Thinking ahead to your next visit, we flew home via North Caicos to check out the Prospect of Whitby, a very new resort hotel—beautifully done inside and out. There, we had our muddy clothes washed, ate lunch and swam in the pool. The young Austrian/English couple who run it (Helmud and Annette) are extremely nice. When Annette heard I hadn't brought a swimsuit with me, she lent me a bikini.

North and Middle Caicos have rolling hills of green, fields of grass, rich soil and dramatic cliffs that drop to miles of vacant white sandy beaches. I love how the sugar-white sands seem to slip beneath a clear layer of ever-deepening turquoise water that reaches out to a crashing white barrier reef and deep-blue ocean beyond.

Mike is staying with us for a few more days before travelling on, so today the three of us went to Six Hills for what we thought would be a relatively routine conch survey. Mike, Chuck and I had just re-entered the water after lunch (sandwiches in the boat) when an enormous manta ray glided past us, silently, gracefully, not more than 10 feet away from us. It seemed to be the size of our living room ceiling (I exaggerate, but that was my impression). It's the first manta I have ever seen in the wild, and to have it swim so close—passing between us and the cay in just 13-or-so feet of water—was truly an awesome surprise. Due to the shallow depth of the study site, I tend to forget that we are nevertheless not far from what they call "the deep." We were spell-bound by this majestic giant and our eyeball-to-eyeball encounter!

*Love, Kathy*

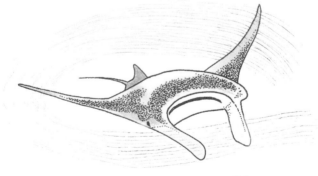

Manta ray

*December 2, 1974*

*Dear Mom & Dad,*

The year is quickly winding to a close, and holiday season is already upon us. We had a lovely Thanksgiving celebration over at Mooney's (Muriel Stubb's) house. Bill Waterworth returned from the States with a huge turkey and cranberry sauce. I baked two 10" pumpkin pies from fresh Haitian pumpkin (green and white outside, orange inside), and I also baked biscuits. There were mashed potatoes, glazed Haitian sweet potatoes (like sweet white tubers), string beans and carrots, avocado tossed salad, potato salad, macaroni and cheese, celery and olives, turkey gravy, banana bread and stuffing. It was quite a feast! The day before Thanksgiving, there were all sorts of people, including myself, floating in and out of Mooney's house all day long, helping to prepare this and that. To get from the road to Mooney's house, each person must wade through an assortment of puppies (her shepherd just had a litter), chickens, kittens and potted plants. She has a sign out front that reads, "Mooney's Zoo." Oh yes, there's also Trevor, the lively one year old of her niece's that Mooney is raising as her own. It is truly a wonderful zoo, and Mooney takes it all in stride.

Meanwhile, Lee Penn is battling a controversy over who will live in the government house that is currently attached to the Department of Fisheries. Tony Rae and his family currently live there, but when Tony finishes his post as Fisheries Advisor and Lee takes over as Fisheries Officer, will Lee and his family get to live there?

Or will it be the government physician who moves in because the house has suddenly become the Doctor's House instead? Lee is the first Fisheries Officer that is a Belonger, not an ex-pat, and the timing of this push to turn the government Fisheries house into the Doctor's house suggests that certain ex-pats are not wanting to relinquish their dominance.

In other news, a lawyer has been down here from the mainland investigating Butch Moody (pilot and former shareholder of WIDL) regarding the 2-5 million dollar (depending on which paper you read) marijuana delivery. Apparently 11 people have been arrested. "Never a dull moment", as Chuck says.

Latest news update: Early this morning, a fisherman delivered five of my tagged conch to the Fisheries office. I found them still alive, sitting in the Fisheries tank. What an exciting surprise! These tagged conchs disappeared from the study site last October. I can't wait to learn more about where they were collected.

*Love, Kathy*

*December 8, 1974*

**Dear Mom and Dad,**

We thoroughly enjoyed your letter. No, we don't need the collecting jars, but please do send down the thermometers! And yes, the huge fish in the photo is Snaggletooth, the barracuda who greets us on every dive at Six Hills—you probably can't see it in the photo, but the tip of his upper jaw is flat and pinkish, exposing two teeth when his mouth is closed, hence, his name.

Speaking of Snaggletooth, here's an update:

After swimming our grid transects, we swam east of the grid to see if we could spot any tagged conch roaming beyond its perimeter. I'd just been congratulating myself on how completely at ease I felt with Snag these days, despite some of his peculiar habits, when we were

approached by an enormous new barracuda that made Snaggletooth look like an innocent pipsqueak. It wasn't that he was so much longer than Snag (about 4.5 feet), but he had a massive girth and teeth like an alligator. After watching him go through his postural displays for our benefit (raising his dorsal fins, snapping jaws and wagging head, but thankfully, no charges), he backed off a bit and we headed back to the boat with him following behind us.

As our anchored boat loomed into view, I saw Snaggletooth's familiar form hanging out in the shadow beneath the hull. He was a welcome sight, for he's very territorial. Whether he chased the visiting 'cuda away, we don't know for sure, because we didn't stop to watch. We just know that by the time we'd removed our dive gear and surfaced at the boat, the big one was gone. I never expected I would *welcome* Snag's presence, but on that day he was definitely my hero.

*Love, Kathy*

*December 30, 1974*

**Dear Mom & Dad,**
We hope you had a wonderful Christmas!

We were planning to give you all a call on Christmas Day, but we never got the chance to get over to the Arms. I'm sure you'll understand when I explain...

We were getting ready to head out the door when an impromptu Christmas party arrived on our doorstep. Julius Jennings and his local band visited our house to bring Christmas cheer, island fashion. (Accordion. Saw. Skin drum. Guitar. Maracas. And plenty of Heinekens in tow!) They settled in for the afternoon in a blissful Heineken haze. Frankie Missik showed up, too. He's a local entertainer who has spent the past five years doing dance/song shows around the Bahamas. Everybody was singing, dancing and improvising songs. It was quite a festive afternoon, and typical of the Caicos holiday season. The amounts of Heineken beer and music that are put away and put forth around town this time of year are prodigious. After an hour and a half and another case of beer, the music and dancing was all in sort of slow motion, and by the time the rather glassy-eyed band members moved along to the next stop down the road, it was too late to make the call.

There have been dances nearly every night, little "junkanoo" bands staging around town, and strings of Christmas lights adorn many of the houses. Lots of good cheer is spread all around. And if you're standing on the beach when the moon is high and you squint your eyes a bit, you might swear you're looking at snow! Happy New Year!

*Love, Kathy*

*January 1975*

**Dear Mom and Dad,**
Today we received the tool kit and your box of goodies.
WOW, SUPER! What fun it is to live where special little
cakes and other goodies are such a treat. Living simply,
as we do, I can much better appreciate the thrilling discovery of nuts and oranges in a stocking on an old Eng-
lish Christmas. The tool kit looks just right—can't wait
to sit down with it, but again we are running a ragged
pace of life and look forward to a future decrease in
tempo…

It was terrific having Alison here! She was a great
dive companion and fellow adventurer. And during her
two-week stay with us, she charmed some of the young
men we go diving with…

One morning, as we were just finishing breakfast,
we heard the rumble of some large vehicle coming
down the road. Such a foreign sound along our quiet
streets called me out to the yard just in time to see our
friend, Jim Shelfant (one of the "Coasties"), driving up to
our house in a big yellow backhoe! Jim beamed down at
us from the backhoe and said he'd come to see if Alison
would like to take a spin around the town. Well, how
many ladies get invited to take a spin in a backhoe?!!
Alison climbed aboard, and off they went. Not too long
thereafter, Alison returned home, alone and on foot.
Apparently Jim had borrowed the Coastguard's backhoe
without permission, and when one of its wheels sank
into a soft patch of road sand and got stuck, she felt it
was a good time to walk herself home.

The same Mackey flight that returned Alison to the States delivered Dr. and Mrs. Schroeder to South Caicos for their collecting expedition. Bob and Jean Schroeder are the parents of green turtle mariculture. They conceived and established the first turtle farm, the Cayman Islands Turtle Mariculture Project. They have long since quit that project, and have freelanced their way around the world using their writing and photography skills. (Bob gave us an autographed copy of his book about marine life and underwater adventures, *Something Rich and Strange*, a fascinating read.) Bob and Jean have come to South Caicos to collect specimens for the American Cancer Institute. They will be here for one month, renting a boat from WIDL, and Chuck and I are the lucky folks who will help them gather specimens. Apparently many coral reef plants and animals contain active compounds that can be used for medical purposes. Our job is to help Bob and Jean collect five pounds each of a broad assortment of common reef organisms that will be sent to the American Cancer Institute for analyses in the lab. It's a "shot in the dark" approach, as Bob says, but that's often how new discoveries are made.

Guess what friends of yours and ours have been invited to cruise the Pacific by sail? Us! The Schroeders have invited us to crew with them next year, if and when they go on a collecting expedition to the Pacific. I say "if," because there is some doubt whether their grant will come through from the American Cancer Institute in light of the present economic crunch. But what a fun thought—and we accepted, of course.

*Love, Kathy*

*March 3, 1975*

**Dear Mom & Dad,**
March is "spring" here, or at least it spells the end of winter storms and the beginning of calm weather. The seagrass in the grid area at Six Hills is beginning to turn green, and the conch population, which shifted away from shore off the grass bed last November, has now shifted back to the grass. The fishermen tell us the conchs, having been "set down" for the winter, will now get up and begin to "walk plenty."

Courting black
damselfish

Other signs of spring are happening on the seagrass beds. Male damselfish are beginning to show their breeding colors and do courtship dances to impress the females. A little male black damselfish has staked out his territory in my study site at Six Hills. He has claimed an empty conch shell that sits in one of the grid squares, and I see him every time I'm doing sweeps across that square. Now that spring has arrived, his black sides have become sprinkled with a lovely bit of "gold dust." He often darts at me to protect his conch shell domain as I pass by, but last week he was preoccupied with more important matters. He allowed me to watch quietly as he performed a wonderful little swoop-and-waggle dance for a female damselfish onlooker.

*Love, Kathy*

*April 3, 1975*

*Dear Mom & Dad,*

A week ago, I received a letter from Dave McCarthey that contained Chuck's $800 salary check for being my project assistant. Last week we also received the address book and grinding parts, and today we received the bobbers and tax forms—thank you very much for all. I have already painted and varnished the bobbers for distribution at Six Hills tomorrow, and will let you know shortly which size is best.

Also today, I received a five-page letter from Dr. Perchard, a longtime underwater field observer of conch and other mollusks in Trinidad and Tobago. In five legal-length pages of tiny print, he expounded upon his conch studies (mostly with fighting conch), describing many fascinating observations. He also included three recently published papers of his on *Strombus gigas* and two other conch species. Ditto a letter from Dr. Berg, who has done research on conch species in the Bahamas and Hawaii. Since I'm already corresponding regularly with a Peace Corps fellow in Belize who is studying conch, I suddenly have an awful lot of letters to write!

At Six Hills, the conchs have been up and walking since March—they're going west. It seemed to us last September that conchs were going east for a short period—perhaps we caught them at the end of their eastward trek. We'll know for sure next fall. Anyway, "westward, westward" is the conch password of the day. The fishermen tell us the conch will stop walking in mid-April or thereabouts.

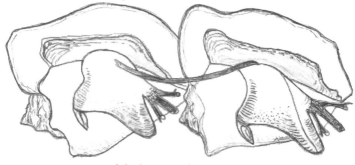

Mating conchs

Conch mating behavior has begun, too, but we haven't seen any spawning yet. When conchs mate, the male approaches the female from behind until the lip of his shell slightly overlaps hers. Under the shelter of their two flared lips, the male extends his "verge" into the female. (A verge is like a black penis that hangs above the male's right eyestalk.) One must flip the two conchs onto their sides to see whether or not mating is actually in process. Much of the time it isn't, but when it is, rolling the pair onto their sides causes the male to quickly withdraw his verge into the safety of his own shell. As he does this, he leaves behind a cloud of fluid that is what I call "electric blue" (bright-cobalt blue). I've tried to get a photo of this, but so far without success. Either we have a camera ready to snap a shot the moment we flip them over, or the pair is mating when we flip them over but we're not ready with the camera; so far we haven't been able to synchronize these two events.

Tomorrow begins a busy week—Monday is a Six Hills day; Tuesday, one of the fishermen is taking us up to the flats and mangroves behind the Coast Guard station to show us where little conchs and lobsters hang out. (He insists there is a breed of pygmy lobster that never grows beyond six inches.) Wednesday, I give another talk about the conch's life history to a church group in town; Thursday, Chuck begins a class in navigation for the locals (at their request); Friday is another Six Hills day again. I think the next five months are going to fly by!

*Love, Kathy*

# The Osprey Incident

"DURING MY TIME IN SOUTH CAICOS, and continuing throughout my life, one of my ongoing passions has been to support, defend, and explore the natural world. The reason I didn't write home about the osprey incident was because my parents were with me when it happened.

Chuck and I were visiting with my family at the Prospect of Whitby, North Caicos. When we arrived, Helmud, Prospect's manager, was overseeing a dredging project to create a

marina behind the hotel. Dredging the channel was in full swing, but trouble was brewing. A conflict erupted over the use of the crane. Two ospreys were determined to make the crane their nesting platform and they were interfering with the dredging job. Helmud and his wife, Anette, favored allowing the ospreys to nest on the crane, and their goal was to complete the channel first. Tom Whiting, owner of Prospect, flew in. I'd

*Opposite page:*
*Top: An osprey carries a large branch to the crane.*

*Bottom: The ospreys stare defiantly from "their" crane.*

*This page:*
*Above and below: The barge with suction pumps arrives from Provo. A team of men and the crane guide it into the channel, where it will begin the next phase of dredging.*

### *The Osprey Incident*

like to say he flew in to oversee the osprey's job, but I suspect his concern was more for the marina. Nevertheless, the rush was on for the crane to complete the channel dredge so the barge with suction pumps could take over dredging the marina, and the ospreys could take over the crane. Did the ospreys succeed in their mission to produce the next generation of ospreys? I never found out, but I like to think so."

*Right: Helmud and his wife, Anette, our hosts at the Prospect of Whitby.*

*Below: Mom and Chris enjoy the pristine beach in front of the hotel.*

Top: At nearby Sandy Point, conch fishermen use poles and a glass-bottom bucket.

Left: At Bellefield Landing, Chris holds a cleaned sponge that sponge fishermen set out to dry.

Below: At Bellefield Landing, Chris and I examine a large sloop under construction.

*Top: Countess Helen Czernin's house on Parrot Cay, viewed from Sandy Point.*

*Left: At Prospect of Whitby, Dad and Chris at the pool.*

*Below: Fisheye view of pool and terrace.*

We accompanied Helmud and Anette to nearby farms that supplied the hotel with fresh produce for our meals.

Above: Farmer Clark shows Chuck and me his vegetable garden.

Below: Anette places an order with Mrs. Delancy outside her store.

*May 3, 1975*

**Dear Mom and Dad,**
April has disappeared so fast I hardly remember it passing.

The Government Fisheries House issue was settled some time ago, as I think you know, with the governor granting Lee Penn permission to live in the Fisheries house as part of his office. Lee is now the islands' first local Fisheries Officer, and he has a list of duties a mile long. He has all the Caicos Islands to inspect and the banks to patrol for poachers. He represents the head of the islands' only industry, and he has a staff of one secretary (and she is on "temporary status") and one boat driver (after nine years' service, Turton is also still "temporary." Lee sent in an application to the governor for an assistant 10 months ago, and his repeated requests for assistance have remained unanswered. If you think there may be something "fishy" going on with the Fisheries here, you're not alone. But without taking pages to tell stories that are probably better off left untold, I'll just say that either these frontier islands attract more than their fair share of people who come here to exploit them and/or strive to build personal empires, or I have just led a very sheltered and idealistic life when it comes to human nature. (I suspect it's mostly the latter.)

There was a recent tragedy here: Jess Mills, the 20-year-old Fisheries mechanic and the older brother of our good friend, Mike Ritchie, died last month while giving some young children piggyback rides in the water. He was ferrying the children on his shoulders, back and forth between the two docks, walking in chest-deep water, when he reportedly collapsed and sank to the bottom just as he delivered the child he was carrying safely to the dock. He just lay on the bottom, and when the children realized he wasn't pretending, they ran screaming to get help. We were out spearfishing with his brother, Mike, at the time (we periodically go fishing with Hawaiian slings to fill our freezer). We returned with our catch to find a crowd gathered on the dock. We saw people administering artificial respiration and cardiac massage to someone lying there. Chuck pitched in on the cardiac massage and was working on the body when he realized it was Jess that he was trying to revive. It was very sad. Jess was a kind and quiet soul. The funeral was the next day.

The sooty and noddy terns have returned to Six Hill Cays, and there's been much chattering and swooping over the water as the noddy terns gather floating sargassum weed to build their nests on the ground and low-lying vegetation of the cays. Below water, there is almost always something new to see as well. Today, while doing surveys in the grid, I came upon something odd sitting out on the grass bed. It was the size of a big fat loaf of bread, golden-brownish like bread, and clearly alive. I picked it up gently—it was rather squishy—and turned it over to look at its underside. The flat underside with many tube feet told me it was an echinoderm, surely some kind of sea cucumber, but of a species I'd never seen before, not even in books. It was covered with protrusions that looked "spiky" but were really as soft as the rest of its body. This "skin" looked similar to a sea cucumber we've seen on night dives that extends the front of its long slender body from beneath a coral head to filter through the sediment. But this thing was short, stout, almost "boxy" and just sitting in the sunshine. I set it down again on the substrate, and that's when the big surprise came... Suddenly, all the protrusions disappeared, the surface skin became smooth, the body shape became more cylindrical, and it began rolling towards me! Yeeks! What on Earth?? I reflexively moved out of its way and watched as it rolled for a good few feet across sand and sparse grass before stopping and resuming its "loaf of bread" shape. What an amazing defense mechanism! I assume I scared it when I picked it up, and its fastest mode of escape wasn't crawling, but rolling. Perhaps it doesn't matter to them which way they roll, since this sudden change of form and motion would startle many predators. It certainly startled me!

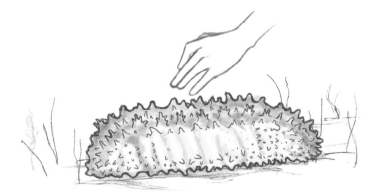

Nellie

Back at Fisheries, we have a new batch of chicks in the yard that run around cheeping and getting lost inside the building by mistake. The Fisheries cat ignores them and continues to press us with her attentions while we are at work. Meanwhile, the cat at our house (she is intent on adopting us; everyone seems to have a cat or two because they keep the mice and roaches in check) has learned how to open the front door by herself. She arrives underfoot as soon as I go to the kitchen to cook dinner. Her sixth sense tells her we've settled down to read a good book, and she's suddenly lap sitting on top of the pages. I'm sure people think we're paranoid because we lock our door a lot during the day, but it's the only way to keep her outdoors. You know how much of a cat lover I am, but this kitty is obsessed with "kneading dough" on every arm or leg she comes in contact with. This wouldn't be such a problem if she would learn to retract her claws!

Even Nellie, the town goat, has decided to be friends with us. She comes running now when we call, and she prances all around, dancing on her hind legs, following us and getting in our way when we walk. She goes bananas for a tasty bit of newspaper, though she won't look twice at a nice patch of grass (she's better than an incinerator). One day she got our neighbor's young dog so jealous by captivating our attentions that the dog tried eating newspaper, too, until he finally left in disgust.

We are getting itchy to go sailing again—the weather is hot and calm these days, and we're getting ready to take *Alondra* to Six Hills for a week of conch-watching and working on the boat. We plan to go and return before the Caicos Regatta, on May 24th.

*Love, Kathy*

PS: I am glad to hear that this last set of bobbers are on their way, but am sorry to have pressured you with the hurry-up note when I know you are busy, too. Chuck and I have had colds for the past week. They have slowed us down enough for me to realize some things just aren't worth getting upset about (most things) and, as Chuck likes to say, "All things come to pass." (Well, not <u>ALL</u> things, I hope.) Anyway, take your time about the list of other items, and scratch off lemonade mix— lemonade powder has just come to South Caicos!

*May 21, 1975*

**Dear Mom and Dad,**
This morning we received the bobbers and yellow paint, tea and swimsuit—all were very gratefully received, too! Tonight we'll hold a big bobber painting session.

We have spent the last five days at Six Hills in *Alondra*—what a lovely interlude. The best parts of our days there were late afternoons when the breeze dies, the ocean calms and the sky turns golden. Frigate birds return from a day's fishing at sea and soar like black kites over the cays, and all is peace and bliss. Enjoying fresh-caught seafood for supper (lobster and conch chowder) is the cherry on top.

We returned yesterday in time to help entertain some of the crew of a British frigate warship on a "flag-showing" tour of the Caribbean—there was an open house at Fisheries, a barbecue on Bell Sound, a tea held at the District Commissioner's house and cricket matches. It was a general holiday for all. We spent part of the afternoon talking conch and other things with the ship's captain. I believe he felt a kinship with Chuck's Annapolis Academy background, for he invited us to ride on the ship with him that evening when they returned a few British government people to Grand Turk. We had to decline the offer, though, as we were tired from our long day, and there would be no return flight on TCA that evening.

Today was the public auction for the three Haitian sloops that were confiscated for carrying marijuana (it was stuffed inside radiators). Glad to report that Bob Parkinson got the sloop he wanted. We will be looking after it for him until further notice.

This weekend will be the Caicos Regatta—boat races, donkey races, water sports, a banquet of local foods at the Admiral's Arms, a "Miss Regatta" contest out by the pool in the evening, music groups, singing and playing, and more. Welcome home to the rush and excitement of South Caicos!

By next week, things will be calm enough to resume Six Hills visits, though the number of tagged conchs still present has now dwindled to about 50. They have gone west, beyond the end of Six Hill Cays (except for the 50 or so), and from that point on it's all open bank. Searching for a tagged conch out there is like playing the needle in a haystack game.

I am anxious to begin tying up the loose ends of my project and outlining my report. I guess it is (or has just finished being) that hectic "end of term" time at the University, but I find it strange that I have not heard a word from Dr. Rankin since February. When he (and Dr. Rich, also on my advisory committee) recommended converting my M.S. program to a Ph.D., he said all I needed to complete my doctorate was one last class, either in language or statistics. I think he was expecting me to jump at this opportunity. Maybe I should have, but when I didn't and gave my reasons, Dr. Rankin sent me a brief note saying he'd reconsidered. I haven't heard from him since. In late February, I sent him a progress report on my Six Hill Cays project, as well as the rough draft of an article I'm writing for publication on the conch "climbing" behavior I observed in the lab, but I've received no response to either of these items. I do hope he is okay.

I know you are itching to ask the ten thousand dollar question: after South Caicos, what then? Well, we don't have a final answer yet. When I received Dr. Rankin's letter encouraging me to convert to a Ph.D., Chuck's response was that if I got mine, he wanted to get his. We began investigating graduate schools at Universities of Miami and Hawaii. Hawaii seems tailor-made, as far as catalog course offerings and professor interests go. There are the usual hassles, including GRE exams that Chuck must take in the States this fall. (They're only given at special times and places.) If graduate school is in our future, it will not be before September '76, a year away, at the earliest.

We have thoroughly enjoyed our time here in South Caicos and our relationship with Lee at Fisheries, so we've contacted the representative at American Consul Carib, searching for similar job opportunities on other (U.S.) islands. We plan to remain here through hurricane season (through October) before moving on.

We received another letter from Bob Schroeder, full of his usual news clippings on the Mid-East situation, lengthy philosophies and dire predictions of doom. He ended on a lighter note, that the specimens they collected from Fiji for the American Cancer Society showed a new record high of 25% activity. He concludes with the hope that "maybe we all still can manage to be somewhere SW of Bora Bora on the coming of the Armageddon..."

Now I have to go—there are two sailboats in the harbor, one from Belgium and the other from Germany. The two couples (Belgian and German) are sailing together and we're going out to visit them now.

*Love, Kathy*

*July 17, 1975*

**Dear Mom and Dad,**

We have some time to ourselves now—the first in weeks without anything extraordinary planned in the immediate future. The past two weeks have seen us entertaining our own "dive group" of three. To explain...

Last year, when Chuck and Bob worked for WIDL, a group of four divers arrived from Detroit (two couples, close friends in their early forties, with underwater photography as a hobby) and spent a lot of time with us. They had such a great time they decided to return for two weeks to dive with us again.

We've all had a packed two weeks of scuba diving, sailing and exploring the caves on Middle Caicos. They particularly enjoyed helping out with the conch project—doing underwater transects throughout the grid area and plotting the positions of conchs using underwater paper and clipboards. Aside from photographing many underwater shots of the conch project, Vern left us with a set of close-up lenses for our Nikonos, an underwater strobe housing with strobe for flash shots underwater, oodles of color film, and an offer to develop all the film for free as we use it up (he develops his own). He gave us two weeks of practice and instruction while he was here. What a gift!

During our time with them, we had several thrill-packed dives off The Wall that included encounters with sharks. One of these involved a 10-foot hammerhead (well, maybe 8-9 feet, but still...) that was attracted to the strobe flash. You really need a flash for good close-ups of reef life at that depth, but sharks are very curious. Every time the flash went off, this hammerhead veered in closer to have a better look. (Needless to say, we're fast learners and didn't keep taking shots for long.)

I'm working backwards in time as I go through our news... Chuck was in Miami and Ft. Lauderdale for four days shortly before the divers arrived; here's what happened.

We were riding out in the Coast Guard van to a party at the base when we encountered Mike Ritchie. He waved us down with one arm as he lay in the middle of the road with a broken leg. He'd been riding his motorbike, heading to the party, when he skidded in a patch of soft sand in the road and fell. That was at 9:15 pm. The leg above his ankle was bent back about 30 degrees at the shin, and Mike told us that when he reached down he'd felt the rough edge of exposed bone.

Then began the long night—driving back to town, finding the nurse and collecting pilots to fly to Grand Turk.

We arrived in Grand Turk at 11:00 p.m., and the doctors there gave Mike some antibiotic shots. I won't give all the details except to say that despite his compound fracture, Mike never even cried—he joked and sang instead. Such a strong boy, I stand in awe. It helped that Chuck did not leave his side for a second and, as the doctors in Grand Turk discussed whether to send him to Puerto Rico, Nassau or Miami, Chuck made sure he would go to Miami where he would be near Bob and Chris (Mike is a good friend of Bob's) and get the best care.

Chuck and I had already decided that Chuck should fly with Mike to Miami to make sure he got medical treatment as fast as possible. I returned to South Caicos at about 1 a.m. while Chuck, Mike's sister, Kay, and a nurse awaited the plane (which had to be called from the States) to travel with Mike to Miami. They didn't arrive in Miami until 8:45 a.m. the next morning, and Mike didn't get the surgery until 10 a.m., having been conscious and in good spirits the whole time.

Chuck called the next afternoon with stories of Emergency Room chaos (imagine the ER at the largest hospital servicing Miami) and endless forms to fill out, but a good outlook for Mike's leg. The leg had gone untouched for 12 hours, but an operation revealed no signs of infection and now, two weeks later, Mike is out of the hospital and staying with Bob and Chris. The prognosis is that his leg will again be as good as new.

Chuck remained in Miami/Lauderdale until the next Mackey flight (Tuesday), staying with Bob and Chris and helping Lee Penn square away some things with the Fisheries patrol boat, *Watchful*. (Lee was in Miami at the time.) Chuck didn't have his wallet or any I.D. on him when he flew with Mike to Miami, but thankfully, under the circumstances, U.S. Customs never stopped to question.

As for me, I have never felt more completely at ease and safe while alone than in South Caicos. No kooks or perverts here, and everybody knows everyone.

Last bit of news: We got a letter from Bob Schroeder yesterday, asking if we were interested in making

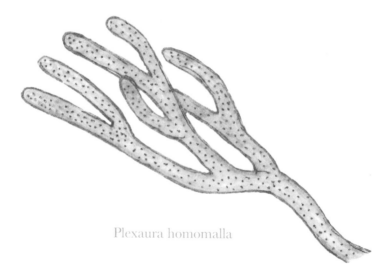

Plexaura homomalla

"a fairly quick $1,000" by collecting 50 kg of a particular species of gorgonian for a medical researcher at the University of Omaha. A man named Dr. Weinhelmer originally discovered the presence of prostaglandin in *Plexaura homomalla*, a common gorgonian. It is being used to develop a birth control pill for men. Apparently the *P. homomalla* found in Florida has the wrong prostaglandin isomer, and so it can't be used.

We said yes and are now awaiting the shipping cans and boxes—oh, yes, and a specimen of *P. homomalla* so we know what we're after.

*Love, Kathy*

# Things I Never Told My Parents
## *(Harrowing stories of small planes and boats)*

ALTHOUGH I SHARED MANY ANECDOTES with my parents about daily life on South Caicos, there were certain events I kept silent about because I knew they would cause my parents too much worry about my welfare. I did share them, however, with my sister, Alison. The following letter to Alison offers some glimpses into the wilder side of life on the Caicos frontier.

*June 1974*

*Dear Alison,*

What an eventful week it's been! A blue sailboat with four people aboard from the Virgin Islands departed from South Caicos last Monday after spending a few days here. That night, they ran smack into a dangerous reef off East Caicos and their ship broke up. The next morning they were spotted in their open life raft, drifting toward the shores of East Caicos. No one on South Caicos (or anywhere else) knew of their shipwreck until a plane—while flying outside of its normal route looking for a different boat that had been reported missing—spotted their raft, purely by accident, and radioed their position to the South Caicos tower. East Caicos is a huge island with no human inhabitants, no airport or runway, but the four survivors were rescued successfully by another small plane that was able to land on the salt flats there. The whole tale is long and fraught with danger and adventure; it is jarring to realize how easily these folks could have died. If the weather hadn't been abnormally calm, their life raft could not have drifted safely through the coastal reef and rocks to shore. If a plane hadn't strayed from its normal route for another purpose, they wouldn't have been spotted. All in all, they are lucky to be alive, well and rescued so quickly. Nevertheless, the boat—their only home, $40,000 and uninsured—was a total loss. Chuck and I joined others in devoting the next two days to search for and salvage what we could find of their shipwrecked belongings.

A couple of days ago there was another incident. A small private plane with three people aboard got lost somewhere north of here and east of the Bahamas. The airport tower picked up the distressed pilot on radio and they talked with him for hours as they tried to determine his position. Other plane pilots were listening, too. A commercial airline pilot went out of his way to spot the small plane. He gave the lost pilot a bearing to follow that would take him to South Caicos, where he could refuel. By that time, though, the plane's supply of gas was too low to make it to South Caicos, and the plane ran out of gas. The pilot was given directions on how to make a belly landing on the sea. The plane had no emergency flares and no life raft. It had nothing other than three life jackets for its three passengers. The last radio communication anyone heard from the small plane's pilot was his voice counting down as the plane lost altitude..."three thousand feet...two thousand feet...one thousand feet..." Silence. The area where the plane went down has been searched for the past two days,

## *Things I Never Told My Parents*

but trying to spot a life jacket in the open sea—if indeed there are or were survivors—is like trying to find a needle in a haystack. What a tragic ending.

Of course, I didn't share this next incident with Mom and Dad, either, but Chuck and I had our own experience of being airborne in a plane when its engine ran out of gas. Here's what happened...

One night, our inflatable dingy went adrift from its mooring. Upon hearing the news, Paul Loughrey, our good friend who flies cargo around the islands, offered to fly us on a search mission over the Caicos Bank the following morning to see if we could spot our lost dinghy from the air. Based on wind direction, he felt there was a chance we might find it blown up against the mangroves somewhere.

At sunrise the next morning, Paul took Bob, Chris, Chuck and me up in the Twin Beech aircraft to search for the dinghy. We'd been airborne for about 30 minutes when I heard one of the plane's two noisy engines suddenly go silent. In that same moment, I saw the propeller on the engine right outside my window come to a full stop. I reflexively looked toward the cockpit at Paul. I saw him turn his head to Bob Parkinson (in the copilot seat), and I read Paul's lips as he yelled above the drone of the remaining engine: "We're out of gas!" Uh-oh. I looked down at the ocean below, knowing we'd be down there shortly, one way or another.

The day was sunny and the ocean was reassuringly calm. I didn't feel scared as much as I felt on high alert. I began reading the directions posted on the emergency exit door so I would know how to open it and exit when the time came. Meanwhile, Paul radioed the airport tower to clear the runway for an emergency landing, and he instructed Bob to

start pumping a manual lever in the cockpit that looked like a bilge pump handle. Fortunately, we were closer to South Caicos than I realized, and we soon landed safely on the runway in the traditional fashion, with one prop still turning. Only after we'd landed safely and I stood up to exit the plane did I notice that my knees were trembling like jelly.

Paul explained that because the plane's gas gauges were unreliable, he had filled up the spare gas tank in the plane's nose the previous evening. He always flew with some extra gas in reserve, and a full nose tank guaranteed our safe return. Apparently, someone had siphoned out that fuel during the night. Bob's manual pumping action had maintained pressure in the gas lines, which helped the system use every last drop of gas to keep the remaining engine running. Thanks to the second engine, it was just a close call.

Actually, close calls of one sort or another seem to happen quite often. Another "plane incident" happened last month when Paul was finishing up a cargo run in the Twin Beech. By the time Chuck, Bob, Chris and I heard the news

*Things I Never Told My Parents*

and arrived at the airport, an anxious group of onlookers was standing in the terminal tower. Some had been there for the past hour as Paul flew in circles overhead, talking with the tower. The plane's landing gear was jammed, and Paul was trying to get the plane's wheels to lower so he could land. We waited anxiously with the others for another 45 minutes as Paul, still airborne and circling, tried jumping on the landing gear compartment at intervals, trying to shake the wheels loose so they would lower into position.

Paul was just to the point of leaving for Grand Turk to make a belly landing on their runway (they have foam there to coat the runway) when the landing gear came partially down. Even though the wheels descended only halfway, Paul was able to make a superb landing. As his plane touched down and taxied, our little crowd spontaneously erupted in a communal cheer of joy and relief!

*Love, Kathy*

When we lived in town, Chuck and I would sometimes hear planes circling overhead at night. We knew this was a sign that someone had to drive out to the airport and turn on the runway lights. The airport closed at 5 p.m., so on the days that Paul made his cargo rounds to the other islands, someone would leave the runway lights on for him because he often returned after dark.

One time, as we accompanied Paul on his rounds, we returned after dusk to find the runway dark. Someone had forgotten to leave the lights on. Rather than fly in circles over the town, and because he was so familiar with the runway, Paul felt confident landing the plane using just the power of the plane's own headlights. First, he made a preliminary low pass to "clear the runway of any donkeys." (Donkeys? I'd never seen a donkey at the airport.) Then he circled in for a landing. As we were approaching touchdown, the plane's headlights lit up the runway brightly in front of us. Having grown up in Connecticut where driving at night along unlit, winding country roads was the norm, I thought nothing of it—until a wild donkey suddenly bolted across the runway right in front of us like a startled deer. It was a good reminder of why well-lit runways prevent accidents and save lives.

*September 8, 1975*

**Dear Mom & Dad**

Things continue fine, just busy as ever!

We spent three weeks doing part-time work at Fisheries, teaching marine biology to a couple of local teens. And today, the collecting equipment arrived from Bob Schroeder so we can commence our gathering of 100 kg of gorgonians. Chuck is committed to teaching four more Coast Guard guys to dive, but this will be his last South Caicos dive class.

One year of fieldwork at Six Hills is now complete. Next week we'll do a night dive and a last checkup on some sub-adult conchs that I put surface tags on—it's really neat to look out across the calm sea surface and see little floats moving steadily onward.

The skiff boat has finally pooped out, but it took a long time dying. The engine has been giving us trouble for months, and the last few weeks saw Chuck tinkering for days after each run to Six Hills just to keep it going— warped head, saltwater in the lower cylinder, sticking brushes on the starter and, last but not least, stripped threads on one of the sparkplugs…not to mention the loose battery connections. (Did my knowledge impress you? I'll never make a mechanic, but I've learned a little something from Chuck's dedicated labor and expertise, without which this project could not have survived.) Thankfully, the engine lasted us almost to the end, and we sailed to Six Hills in *Alondra* for the final few days to finish up. We just sailed home yesterday, thoroughly POOPED, and we gave another slide show at Mooney's last night.

We are planning to spend the last of my University grant money for gas and miscellaneous funds on new parts for the Fisheries skiff boat engine. We want to leave it in running condition, as we found it, and there's no money left in the Fisheries kitty after the unexpected sums that were spent to fix the *Watchful*.

Most of my time from now on will be devoted to preparing my research report, and Chuck's to studying for GREs, interspersed with dive classes and collecting specimens of *P. homomalla* (with all the attendant tank charging and compressor maintenance), not to mention scraping, hauling and painting Bob Parkinson's sloop in return for the many work-related favors Bob has done for us in Ft. Lauderdale. We did our own boat last month—two-and-a-half days of dawn-to-dusk work—but the good part was we could work while standing in cool ocean water. (Can't do that at a shipyard!)

*Love, Kathy*

*September 10, 1975*

*Dear Chris,*

You were in my dream last night, and we were having lots of fun. I dreamed we were outdoors at some kind of a party. There were lots of happy people around us, and we all played games. We ran around a lot and then we ate gigantic marshmallows!

The funniest piece of news I want to share with you is this: Last summer, a friend of mine named Mooney bought a baby pig. Mooney is a really nice lady who loves animals. She already has three big dogs and six puppies, two cats and four kittens, lots of chickens, two roosters and a cute little baby boy named Trevor. Last year, she made a sign that hangs in her yard. It says "Mooney's Zoo" because there are always lots of people and animals at her house. Her pig's name is Bert. Here's what's funny—Bert thinks he is a dog. Bert is about three months old now (the size of a little dog) and he thinks the puppies are his brothers and sisters. When a stranger comes to Mooney's door, the dogs all

bark and Bert rushes up oinking with them. Bert comes when he is called and scratches at the door to be let in (even though Bert and the dogs are not allowed inside the house). I went to Mooney's house last week to visit her. As we stood talking in her yard, a puppy came up to play. He chewed and tugged at the leg of Mooney's pants, hoping to get her attention. Next thing I knew, Bert ran up to Mooney. He started chewing and tugging at her *other* pants leg.

*Love, Kathy*

*September 19, 1975*

*Dear Mom & Dad,*

A quick note to say we all survived the hurricane scare. After all the initial excitement and flurry of preparing for the big blow—moving boats, setting extra anchors and lines, boarding up and closing shutters, collecting extra water, etc. etc.—a high pressure ridge sent Hurricane Eloise to the south of us, and we never received more than 40-50 mph winds. Thank heavens for that! As caretakers of Bob Parkinson's sloop and our own, we weren't eager for the excitement or catastrophe of a big storm. As it is, the cement hotel dock crumbled away, and Bill Waterworth's dock and mooring pond has changed shape completely. It's now about half the size it was, with a solid bank around it—no exit. The shorefront has shifted around all the way down the line, but no serious damage was done to boats or homes.

Anyone inland would have thought the whole thing passed by smoothly with little ado, but the shorefront was a chaotic scene the day before Eloise was due to hit. The harbor area was crammed with boats—two Haitian sloops, some island cargo boats, a few local sloops, *Alondra*, a yacht in transit... Tied to the pier were an old wooden fishing vessel 85 feet long and a yacht that was tied alongside the 85-footer. (The "yacht" was a 45-foot sailboat; all foreign sailboats are called "yachts" here; yep, even our 28-foot wooden ketch with no engine!) Having spent the morning readying our own boat as much as we could as well as Bob's boat, we stopped by to see how the 45-foot yacht was doing. She had three guys aboard who had never been on a sailboat before. These three were serving as her crew. Her captain was away on business, and the crew didn't know *what* to do. Ditto the 85-foot vessel; her captain was absent as well, leaving three land-lubber crewmen aboard with only two tiny anchors, one functional engine out of two, and a punky (with wood rot) wooden hull that leaked even in fair weather. Rumors were swirling about why this vessel had come here in the first place, expecting to receive a fishing license. Whether it be a front for smuggled cargo, fishy fish-dealings, something Mafia managed or all three, no one here has much sympathy for it.

Chuck gave the yacht crew some advice before we headed home to make preparations there—moving everything off our screened front porch, and placing heaps and piles of stuff up off the floors and out from under major leak sites in the roof. We returned to the harbor area in time to see a huge Bahamian trader arrive to drop some cargo. The 85-footer had to leave the pier to make room for the trader to unload. The 85er tried to move with the yacht still tied to her side, thinking she could steer them both. (The yacht has a tiny engine and wanted the free ride.) Both boats rapidly headed for Bob's moored sloop, at which point the yacht let itself loose and motored away, but the 85er steered right into Bob's boat and wrapped its prop around one of our anchor lines, slicing it in two. In no time, we had our dinghy alongside them, and Chuck was overboard cutting away the line fouled in the prop. Bob's boat was unhurt, and the 85er was now resting against an anchored Haitian sloop.

The 85er's three crewmen were distraught and urged Chuck to pilot them through the anchored boats to deep water. So we climbed aboard and Chuck took the wheel, barking orders, while I talked to the big waggy New-foundland doggy on deck. There was no relay system between the wheelhouse in front and the engine room in the stern, so each command had to be relayed from one man to the next. We tried anchoring, but the anchors were of no use, made for a boat not much bigger than ours. As an alternative to anchoring, Chuck pointed out an area of deep water in which they could putter in cir-cles safely until the Bahamian vessel left the pier. Once the Bahamian vessel moved off, he explained, the 85er could return to the pier. (In a bad storm, the 85er, tied to the pier, would surely destroy either herself or the pier, but probably better to sink near shore than be strewn across the bank.) Actually, the crew had no idea they might sink; they just had no idea of anything, and they became despondent when Chuck refused to steer them around for two hours until the Bahamian vessel left and then take them in to the pier himself.

We left the 85er to its circles and returned to Bob's boat to set a new anchor line. We finished just at dusk. By that time, it looked as if Eloise would pass south of us. Thank goodness. Maximum expected winds: 75 knots. Still plenty strong but could have been so much worse.

The threesome on the yacht were doing fine, having re-anchored in a good spot with a special mooring rig recommended by their captain over the phone. They intended to sleep aboard and come ashore the next morning. We persuaded them not to "ride it out" at anchor, just in case their anchor dragged, because if it *did* drag, they would have no one to rescue them, and nothing but the vast Caicos Bank to be pounded against. They were easily persuaded.

We ate a quick supper and hurried up to Fisheries to prepare for the storm up there. It was pitch dark outside by then, and we found Lee peering intently out the window toward the entrance to the harbor. Following his gaze, we saw the running lights of a large yacht (sailboat, not a power yacht) nosing her way slowly to the northeast of Dove Cay straight toward Tucker Reef. (The harbor entrance is southwest of Dove Cay—between Dove and Long Cay.) The yacht clearly did not know her way and was in danger of being thrown onto Tucker Reef, if she wasn't in fact already upon it! Alas, neither navigational light on either side of the harbor entrance was working. Luckily, a small tug in the harbor saw her at the same time that we did, and it shone a powerful searchlight beam back and forth alternately on Dove Cay and Long Cay, showing her the channel. She immediately shifted course by 90 degrees and made a safe anchorage. Whew!

It was past 11 p.m. when we finally crawled into bed. No one slept well that night. The wind was a brisk 30-35 knots with plenty of hard-driving rainsqualls. It was cold during the squalls (put on a top sheet) and hot between squalls (throw the sheet off again), back and forth all night.

The morning weather promised no more than 60 knot winds—not bad at all compared to what it could have been—and we hurried over to the Arms to check on the boats and see how all were getting along. Norman Saunders's sloop had dragged anchor during the night and was a small but visible spot on the Bank. The Bahamian trader was still parked at the pier, and the 85-footer continued to steam in weary circles. It wasn't long before the trader finished her dockside business and moved out to anchor. At last, the 85er could take her place at dockside. We waited expectantly for the harrowing scene of the ship coming in alongside the dock, but by now she wasn't moving. She had run aground.

The weather remained sunny with scattered squalls, but the wind had kicked up the seas appreciably. It wasn't long before the 85er's crew abandoned their vessel to its own fate, preferring the safety of shore. They came practically two miles to shore in the other threesome's little dinghy.

The rubber dinghy was awash by the time they all arrived, and its engine died shortly after they unloaded.

Except for some fast action and good teamwork involved in hoisting the Fisheries skiff boat from the boiling seas to the dock and then to shore, we passed the rest of the day at the hotel in lively chatter amid lots of pots of tea. Despite the wind, the dramatic seas and high tides, the weather was better than anyone expected, and the sun shone brightly all afternoon.

To those living inland, this was just a sunny day with a stiff wind. When Helen (the VSO teacher from Scotland) arrived from town and commented that the storm was a bit anticlimactic after all the scare and preparations, we all walked out to the veranda and watched as the waves proceeded to smash the dock away. We felt the sting of salt on our faces, and it reminded me of when Alison and I were kids, running from the Weekapaug Inn to the beach to watch the big waves rushing up to the dunes after an early '60s hurricane had passed nearby.

We returned to the hotel after supper—our power being out—and listened to Jack Riley tell stories of fishing the North Sea. Other than a short intermission, during which Chuck and two other men dashed out to help re-moor two small boats that had gone adrift, the evening passed uneventfully.

Today, the sea looks innocently upon the changed waterfront, showing nothing more than a typical winter chop. Norman's boat and the 85-footer still sit on the horizon. We set to work un-boarding shutters at home and at the Fisheries office, hauling bags of dried and smelly *P. homomala* out of the closet, clipping their long fronds into sprigs and packing them for shipment. We dropped by the hotel only long enough to check on the boats and see how people were doing. Bill Waterworth's small dock area was still closed in solid, but three locals— McCoy, Ball Joint and another lobsterman—were now chopping away with shovels and pickaxes to cut a channel through which they could pass their boats, which were kept in the same lagoon. Bill sat watching them from the side. As we came near he muttered glumly, "That won't be big enough for *my* boats; we need dynamite and a hydraulic pump. I've got 10 NAUI dive instructors coming in 10 days."

From the 45-foot sailboat that had anchored safely after its near miss with Tucker Reef in the dark came a dinghy laden with hippy-types from five years old to 50. On board were five kids, five adults and three dogs, all bound for the Virgin Islands where they planned to set up a daycare center.

We didn't stay long enough to inquire about damages farther down the line—like how the missionary boat, *Blessed Hope*, fared during the storm. For the past couple of months, she's been moored at the dock near the fisheries plants with a family of seven living on board. Her flaking ferro-cement hull is as tall as it is wide, and mounted in the hull are big (BIG) square glass windows that sit just two feet above sea level. One day the father, who was also the skipper, asked Chuck if he thought some sails could be put on the thing to make it go faster. He said he and his family were bound for the Virgins—at least that was his plan.

I marvel that the number of accidents at sea isn't much greater when I see how many folks go to sea, believing it's merely a question of putting a house on pontoons with an engine behind it. (Reminds me of a family that got rescued—fortunately!—after getting lost at sea. They were trying to sail south to the Caribbean using a compass and a placemat to navigate by.)

Well it's now 10 p.m., Chuck's falling asleep at his desk, and it's time to leave Fisheries and go home. Chuck says to tell you both and Chris that as we walked past Mooney's last night, there was Bert oinking madly at us through the gate, telling us to keep out, like the good watch-pig he is.

*Love, Kathy*

*Barclay's Bank.*

*I'm standing with Chuck and my brother, Chris, on the front steps of the Admiral's Arms.*

Above: Waterfront. Right-to-left: Custom's House--once a salt shed, now the South Caicos Library; Sail and Salt Building (TISCO); and Cleo Durham's Salt Shed (with peak roof of Fisheries Office visible above it). Gov't Guest House stands on the point.

Left: Lighthouse with District Commissioner's Residence in background.

Below: Kersteiner's salt shed looking toward Government School and Community Center at the end of West Street.

*Above: Overview of buildings along North Street, from St. George's Anglican Church on the right, to the prominent Caicos Holding Company (Stubbs Building) on the left. The blue walls and red shutters of Barclay's Bank can be seen left of center. Photo was taken from the Fisheries Office balcony (2nd floor of the Government Fisheries Building).*

*Below: Walking down North Street from our house towards the harbor. On the left is Caicos Holding Company, Ewing's Store, Barclay's Bank, Anglican Church.*

*Top: District Commissioner's house on the hill behind TISCO building (Sail and Salt Building). More salt piles on left.*

*Above:Government Fisheries Building and a large salt pile, viewed from the intersection of Front Street and North Street.*

*October 11, 1975*

**Dear Mom and Dad,**
The *Plexaura homomalla* has now all been boxed and sent off, Chuck's last dive class is over, and we're now in pretty good shape. Fewer loose ends remain...like what to do with the collection of items we've gathered and have been holding for the eventual materialization of a nature museum. Don't know if I mentioned it earlier or not, but a year ago, there were plans for a little nature museum in town. Government funds had been allotted and all was ready to be put into action to construct it. For the past year, we have been collecting such items as shells, pressed seaweed and coral specimens, plus an array of old artifacts to display reflecting island history. Now we have a room full of neat stuff and nowhere to display it.

The funds for the museum were taken back by England because they were not used in time and the deadline expired. Six months ago a National Parks Committee

was drawn up, but the chairman has yet to call the first meeting; I doubt it will happen. So sad. I wish I knew a magic formula for lighting the fire of enthusiasm in others so they can appreciate and cherish the incredible natural resources that exist here!

Meanwhile, we've received another job offer, one that would keep us in the Caicos. Liam Maguire and some new owners of the Meridian Club operation on Pine Cay are looking for someone to give a hand in setting up and operating a dive outfit there. They are interested in one that's education-oriented so that groups of students could come down for study during the off-season. Wow.

We've already met Bill and Ginny Cowles, new owners of the Meridian Club, and they seem to be genuinely interested in and committed to developing Pine Cay in a way that is low key and environmentally sustainable. In terms of guests and services at the hotel, they are interested in quality over quantity, and they believe Pine Cay could become a showcase for alternative forms of energy such as wind and solar. Chuck tells me he mailed you their new brochure and flyers. Their hearts are certainly in the right place, and I feel the four of us would get along very well. My biggest concern is that they seem as green and idealistic as we were when we came here two years ago. So how their dream actually unfolds as the rubber meets the road remains to be seen. We are waiting to learn more about the exact terms of business before adding this to our pot of possibilities under serious consideration. Of course, we'll keep you posted.

In other news…there was an attempted armed bank robbery last week—the first in Caicos history! Apparently, three boys wearing masks held up her car as Dora Lightbourne was driving from the airport into town with the locked cash box beside her on the seat.

Once a week, the cash box is flown over from Grand Turk in the morning and returned by air at the end of the day so our local Barclay's Bank can do its business. (You remember that cute blue house with the red shutters?)

Barclays Bank

Each week, Dora picks up the cash box at the airport and drives it into town. On this particular day, three local boys took wooden 2 x 4s that were spiked with nails (nails pointing upward that could puncture tires) and laid them across the road in a rather isolated spot between the airport and town. When Dora spied the planks and slowed down to a stop, one of the youths brandished a gun (two of the boys might have had guns; stories conflict) and ordered her to hand over the cash box. Due to amazing skill and cunning on the part of the police, within a few hours all three boys were arrested and the money was retrieved safely. Well, maybe not such amazing skill and cunning was needed after all. The police were helped by the fact that one boy left his jacket (with his name in three-inch lettering across the back) at the scene of the crime. Another boy left his cap (the same one he's been wearing around town for the last month). The boy who did all the talking didn't try to disguise his voice. So, after the robbery, Dora simply proceeded into town, reported the stick-up to the police, and identified the three youths she thought were involved. Oh yes, about the money. In their haste to make off with the dough, the boys forgot to tell Dora to hand over the key to the cash box! Not knowing quite what to do with the heavy, locked box, the boys carried it over to a nearby stone wall and hid it in a shallow hole they dug hastily at its base. They failed to notice a man who was working on the wall some distance away—but he noticed them as they were burying the box. The box was soon recovered, intact. Their trial is today—in progress as I write you. It will be interesting to learn what their sentences are.

And now I can tell you!

As I was writing the above account, Chuck and I began to hear a commotion in the distance. We couldn't tell if it was yelling or cheering; it seemed to be a bit of both. Chuck went out to investigate and he returned with this news: The trial is over and the boys are free to go! In response to this surprising outcome, the boys' teenage friends and peers began to cheer in celebration, while some of the more mature folks responded with howls of outrage that the boys should suffer no consequences for their actions. No one disputed what the boys had done, but apparently they had bungled their job so thoroughly that it was treated as something on a par with a Halloween prank. Sure sounded like one.

*Love, Kathy*

*November 21, 1975*

**Dear Mom and Dad,**

Just a quick note to tell you we've accepted the job on Pine Cay. We will be moving there around the beginning of December, but we will be flying over there this weekend for Thanksgiving to meet some of the other Meridian Club members and take them all snorkeling. Bill and Ginny Cowles are extremely nice. They fly us back and forth in their little Helio Courier, a special STOL aircraft that can take off in the space of a football field and slow to a speed of 45 mph without falling out of the sky.

As you can guess, I have oodles more to tell you about what's in store, but between now and December I must occupy myself with my paper in every spare moment. With the never-ending stream of interruptions that are part of life here, it is difficult to maintain a high-powered train of thought on my thesis, and I want the paper to be 100% up to snuff. All my biologist contacts want copies of it, and thankfully the fellow in Miami who buys conch meats from the Caicos is enthusiastic enough to have offered to xerox as many copies as we need for free. District Commissioner Malcolm has made an appointment for us to speak with the new Chief Secretary about Fisheries affairs tomorrow in Grand Turk, so it's time for me to close.

*Love, Kathy*

PS: Please tell Chis we really enjoyed his last letter and I'll be writing him again soon. And tell him that

Bert the pig is now tossing rocks in the air and retrieving them himself!

*Love, Kathy*

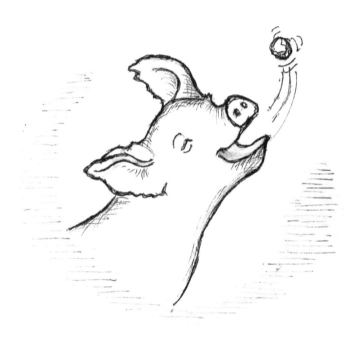

*December 1, 1975*

**Dear Mom and Dad,**

These last few days have been a blur of hurry and flurry… Bart and Marianne are having us over for a special "bon voyage" turtle dinner at the Arms tonight (our last night on island), and Lee and Margaret held a terrific goodbye party at the Fisheries house for us with all our friends; there was dancing and music…the works! This impending departure might feel sadder and more permanent if we were leaving the Caicos altogether, but we're basically just moving down the road apiece. Meanwhile, new adventures are calling us forward. The ironic thing is that on the one hand, we seem to be moving to a different world, at least by Caicos standards, and yet on the other hand, the actual distance of our relocation is just 40 miles away in the same archipelago. So, our Caicos saga will continue for a while yet, but from a new home base.

By some incredible stroke of good luck, the *Zingara*, a small (U.S.) freight boat, showed up in the harbor two days ago, bound for Provo and then Pine Cay. What serendipity! We loaded 41 cardboard cartons of our ever-expanding collection of stuff aboard her. *Alondra*'s cabin is filled with boxes, too, but she's just holding the overflow: bulky items and foodstuffs such as food from our fridge and kitchen cupboards to eat en route, pieces of self-steering vane not yet assembled, and four hand-carved, hand-painted toy native sloops with cloth sails, flopping booms and string rigging that seems to grab at everything that passes within reach.

There's something exciting about setting sail for a new destination; it has an entirely different feel from day sailing. In day sails, you just head out a ways and then return home to the same spot. Even if it's an overnight, you return to the same home base. Cruising to a new destination carries more of a sense of adventure, of voyaging; even if it's short, it's still a journey. We're planning to sail south of Long Cay and then head west across the Caicos Bank, probably anchoring off the tip of Provo for the night. Weather permitting, we'll swing around the north tip of Provo next day and head to windward until we reach Leeward Going Through. We'll spend the night at Leeward and then sail from there, inside the reef, to Pine Cay. It's a three-day journey if the weather cooperates.

Gotta take a shower and get dressed for dinner now. I'll leave this letter at the Arms tonight so it can go out with the hotel's mail. Hope you are all doing well. I'll be in touch at the other end of our trip. Signing off from South Caicos—

*With much love, Kathy*

# The Heart of Conch Country

AS THIS BOOK WAS ABOUT TO GO TO PRESS, I received a package of slides of South Caicos that I thought I'd lost for good.

These old photos, taken by Chuck and me, bring me full circle to the day *Alondra* sailed into Cockburn Harbour in March of 1974—the day I read *The Caicos Conch Trade* and learned of the historic contributions to Caribbean culture and geography made by sailing ships transporting dried conch among the islands. At the time of our arrival in '74, I dubbed South Caicos *the heart of conch country*. Exports of frozen conch from South Caicos to Miami were booming, fishing conch by "hooking"

*Left and below left: At a conch and lobster processing plant, workers prepare fresh conch meats to be boxed, frozen and flown to Miami.*

*Above: In the olden days, a conch fisherman's tools of the trade were a boat with sculling oar, a "water glass" to view the sea bottom, a hooked pole to snag the conch—and plenty of skill.*

*Opposite page top: Conch meats are drying in the sun aboard two boats anchored behind a bank of low shrubs at Conch Ground. Notice the embankment is composed of empty conch shells.*

*Opposite page bottom: A conch fisherman "knocks" his catch of hooked conchs before tossing the empty shells overboard.*

*Right: A large Haitian trading sloop, loaded with dried conch.*

## *The Heart of Conch Country*

was a common sight, and the historic Caicos conch trade was still much in evidence. These photographs capture the flavor of that time. Now, as I gaze upon the graceful forms of the wooden sailing sloops on these pages—some racing at the 1975 South Caicos Regatta, others resting beneath their cargos of dried conchs—I feel grateful to have sojourned in the heart of conch country in time to witness the last days of a passing era when sailing crafts still ruled the local seas, and sun-dried queen conch was still king.

Julius Jennings was a highly skilled fisherman who supplied dried conchs to Belongers and visiting traders.
Left: Julius, Lillian, and 3 of their 20 children pose with me in front of their home.
Below left: Rows of conchs are strung up to dry in front of Julius's house at Conch Ground.

Above: Onlookers watch the races and socialize near the Queen's Parade Ground.

Opposite page top: The Government Fisheries patrol boat, Watchful, referees a race of small sailboats.

Opposite page bottom: Cheering children encourage the rider during a donkey race.

Right: Two of the larger boats prepare for the race to come.

# About the Author

KATHERINE ORR has authored and illustrated twenty-four books, mostly for children. Her award-winning books include *My Grandpa and the Sea* and *Story of a Dolphin*, published by Lerner Books. Her other published writings include grant-funded booklets and articles in professional journals and popular magazines.

Katherine's original book illustrations have appeared in exhibits, including The Society of Illustrator's "The Original Art," at the Museum of American Illustration, New York City; Olympia & York's art exhibition featuring Children's book illustrations at Park Avenue Atrium, New York City; and "The Illustrators Art," at The Dairy Barn SE Ohio Cultural Arts Center. Most of her original book art now resides at the Northeast Children's Literature Collection, University of Connecticut. Her commissioned artworks have ranged widely from scientific illustrations to cartoons, sketches to wall murals, and from the queen conch on a Florida state highway sign to the spiny lobster on a Belize one-dollar bill.

Katherine holds a B. A. in biology, *cum laude*, from Goucher College and a M.S. in zoology from the University of Connecticut, with additional graduate studies in food science at the University of Hawaii, and aquaculture training at National Marine Fisheries Service in Galveston, TX. She holds a certificate in plant-based nutrition from eCornell and the T. Colin Campbell Center for Nutrition Studies.

For more about Katherine and her work, visit katherineshelleyorr.com.

K. ORR

Juvenile pufferfish

Queen triggerfish

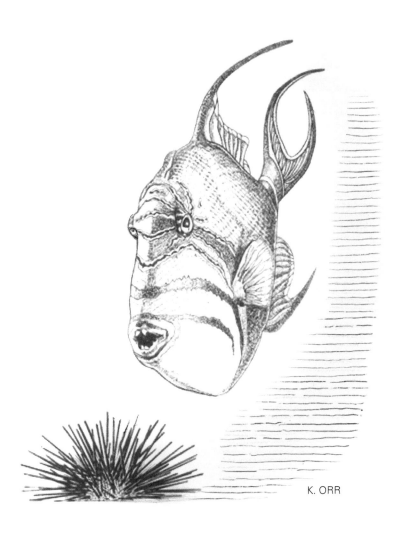

K. ORR

Lightning Source UK Ltd.
Milton Keynes UK
UKHW051933210223
417424UK00004B/132